on track ...
Blur

every album, every song

Matt Bishop

sonicbondpublishing.com

Sonicbond Publishing Limited
www.sonicbondpublishing.co.uk
Email: info@sonicbondpublishing.co.uk

First Published in the United Kingdom 2022
First Published in the United States 2022

British Library Cataloguing in Publication Data:
A Catalogue record for this book is available from the British Library

ISBN 978-1-78952-164-1

Typeset in ITC Garamond & ITC Avant Garde
Printed and bound in England

Graphic design and typesetting: Full Moon Media

on track ...
Blur

every album, every song

Matt Bishop

sonicbondpublishing.com

Acknowledements

I dedicate this book to Adrienne. Thank you for convincing me I could do it, and for your constant encouragement, support and assistance in helping me get started.

Thanks also go to my family for putting up with all the Blur music that blared, blasted and boomed out of my room back when I was a spotty youth in the 1990s. I'd also like to express my gratitude to Stephen Lambe for allowing me this amazing opportunity. Finally, much appreciation and respect to Damon, Graham, Alex and Dave for all the wonderful music, providing the soundtrack to my teenage years and other fond memories.

on track ...

Blur

Contents

Introduction: Seymour (1988-1990)

Like so many classic British groups of the rock era – The Who, Pink Floyd, Roxy Music and Queen, to name just a few – Blur's formation can be traced back to art school: namely Goldsmiths College in New Cross. A constituent of the University of London, the college offers prestigious courses in art, design, music and language with world-famous alumni, including artist Damien Hurst, fashion designer Vivienne Westwood and filmmaker Steve McQueen.

It was here in 1987, whilst studying for a fine art degree, that freshman guitarist Graham Coxon first met Bournemouth-born bass player Alex James, who was reading French. Sharing the same halls of residence, they quickly became firm buddies, bonding over their love of guitars, bands and booze.

As the relationship developed, Graham regaled his newest pal with stories of an extroverted friend from his hometown: singer, songwriter, keyboardist and part-time Goldsmith's music course attendee Damon Albarn. Damon and Graham had been close since the early 1980s, when together they attended Stanway Comprehensive School in Colchester, Essex. Both formally trained musicians, the two boys frequently collaborated on various projects throughout their adolescence, and now – grown up and living in London – played together in a Damon-fronted group called Circus. Also in Circus was computer programmer and drummer Dave Rowntree: an acquaintance of Graham's from Colchester's tiny live music scene.

At some point towards the end of 1988, Graham introduced Alex to Damon, and a hedonistic social bond grew between the young students. Before long, Alex had joined Circus, with the four-piece soon changing their name to Seymour, after the J. D. Salinger novella *Seymour: An Introduction*.

Thanks to a fortuitous arrangement with Euston-based recording studio The Beat Factory – where Damon worked as a tea boy – Seymour were permitted use of the studio at night for free. There they recorded demos with the assistance of studio manager and engineer Graeme Holdaway. In 1989, they recorded a bunch of songs, including 'Fried', 'Shimmer', 'Long Legged' and 'Dizzy'. Though amateurish and stylistically undefined, the recordings demonstrated an intense raw potential that pricked up the ears of Food Records' Andy Ross, who had received a tape Damon had sent. Founded in 1984 by keyboardist Dave Balfe, ex of The Teardrop Explodes (who later added Ross as partner), Food began life as an independent label, subsequently gaining financial investment from EMI towards the end of the decade. The pair promptly began attending Seymour gigs around the capital's pubs and small clubs in late-1989/early-1990. Despite poor attendance – not to mention the guys often being chaotically drunk – Balfe and Ross were impressed by their good looks, charismatic stage presence and unusually accomplished musicianship.

Having courted the group for a number of months, Food eventually offered them a deal on the condition that they change their name. With the label reckoning Seymour to be the moniker of a 'sad indie anorak' band, a long list of alternatives was drawn up – including Sensitize, The Shining Path and Whirlpool. Eventually, Blur was chosen. Signing in March 1990, for the paltry sum of £5000, the young managerless group set off on the long and winding road to world domination. And what an incredible journey it was to be.

Leisure (1991)

Personnel:
Damon Albarn: lead vocals, keyboards
Graham Coxon: guitars, backing vocals, drums (uncredited)
Alex James: bass
Dave Rowntree: drums, percussion
Recorded: May 1990-March 1991
Studios: The Roundhouse, Battery and Maison Rouge
Producers: Stephen Street, Mike Thorne, Steve Lovell, Steve Power, Blur
UK Release date: 27th August 1991, US Release date: 24th September 1991
Label: Food/Parlophone (UK), SBK (US)
Chart Placings: UK: 7, US: did not chart

Upon signing with Food Records, it was decided the best plan of attack for the newly-christened Blur would be to build up a *vibe* by gigging outside of London, thus bolstering the rookie performers' live experience whilst placing them tentatively under the radar of the national music press. Bagging representation from booking agent X-Ray, their first gig billed as Blur was at Brixton Academy on 27 February 1990 supporting Mega City Four and The Cramps. A smattering of UK shows followed over the coming months before the debut single 'She's So High' was finally released in October. Though the track – produced by Steve Lovell and Steve Power – reached a respectable top-50 chart showing, follow-up recordings of 'Bad Day' and 'Close' with the duo were scrapped, leaving Food bosses Dave Balfe and Andy Ross scratching their heads as to whom the boys should collaborate with next.

Fortunately, the band were approached by ex-The Smiths producer Stephen Street, and despite a seven-month lull between releases, his production of the second single 'There's No Other Way' unexpectedly propelled Blur into the big time. An integral player in the Blur story, Street's early recollections reveal a band high on ambition and talent but low on confidence and direction. He told *Uncut* in 2009:

> I remember Graham was quite shy. When we were in the studio, he wouldn't play in the control room with me, he'd sit bunched up in the corner by his amp. Damon, on the other hand, was an extrovert, but he was insecure about his voice back then. He always wanted to double-track it and have reverb, like Lennon. In both cases, they didn't start off as confident as they became later on in life.

This lack of poise coupled with Food's vicelike grip on the choice of material recorded meant the finished album was an incoherent hotchpotch, recorded piecemeal over ten months, with no less than four different producers involved – Madchester-influenced commercial dance-rock sat uneasily alongside thrashing My Bloody Valentine-esque indie guitar noise, while a 1960s psychedelic pop aesthetic (inspired by Damon and Grahams' childhood love of The Beatles and Syd Barrett-era Pink Floyd) hovered over it all like a trippy ghost.

Nevertheless, when released towards the end of summer 1991, *Leisure* flew proudly into the UK albums top 10. Reviews were mixed, but the huge success of 'There's No Other Way' – coupled with the band's growing live reputation (culminating in a well-received August performance at Reading Festival) – ensured that the record had impressively sold nearly 100,000 copies by the end of the year, later earning gold-disc status.

Though Food were delighted with their young new signings, a level of frustration began to creep in among the band members, with them feeling that the album didn't represent who they were collectively or the direction they were headed in. Both Damon and Alex have expressed regret over the exclusion of more esoteric material that ended up as B-sides, correctly assessing that the presence of 'Interia', 'Luminous', 'Mr Briggs' et al. would've made for a much more rounded body of work. Damon's lyrical prowess on the album has also been singled out for derision: an aspect of his songwriting that was to vastly improve in the near future.

However, *Leisure* certainly has its moments, and to call it a bad album would be a mistake that severely overlooked the undeniable promise that shines through from the talented young musicians. They would do much better next time.

'She's So High' (Albarn, Coxon, James, Rowntree)

Double A-side single b/w 'I Know'; Released 15 October 1990; UK: 48

And so begins Blur's fantastic voyage. The debut single was also the first song they ever wrote together, and to this day, is their most democratically-conceived composition.

It's March 1989, and the fledgling Seymour are in rehearsal, jamming around a three-chord sequence of D, C, and A, initiated by Alex. Graham adds a few guitar embellishments and some verse lyrics, while Damon provides a chorus. Done.

Fast-forward to the following year and the summer of Italia '90. The band are now signed to Food Records, and find themselves recording 'She's So High' and 'I Know' at Willesden's Battery Studios: the same venue where The Stone Roses cut 'Fools Gold'. The boys would've found this fact to be particularly fitting, seeing as the 'She's So High' guitar opening bore such a cheeky resemblance to the riff at 3:05 in the Stone Roses' 'I Wanna Be Adored'. But progress was slow.

Being Blur's first professional recording session, producers Lovell and Power were dubious of the young musicians' instrumental chops, insisting on making loops of as many parts as possible. No matter – despite its lyrical simplicity and bandwagon-chasing blend of shoegaze and baggy (a genre that featured predominantly Manchester-based indie dance-rock bands of the late 1980s and early 1990s, wearing baggy jeans and brightly coloured casual tops), the recording was an amorphous, swirling triumph. Alex was even convinced the song would hit number 1.

Landing on the UK singles chart at 48 – not bad for a debut – the track showcased promising hallmarks of the upcoming debut album: Graham's psychedelic backwards guitars; Alex's busy yet languidly-groovy bass and Damon's ear for a catchy chorus cunningly espousing the most basic of impulses: 'She's so high / She's so high / I want to crawl all over her.'

Six years after the single's release, Damon seemed to have finally figured out who the track was meant for. He spoke to *Melody Maker*'s Everett True in 1996: "She's So High' is a classic Oasis song, three years before they appeared. Liam could sing that really well.'

With its mid-paced lumbering groove, distorted strummed guitar chords and narrow, hypnotic vocal melody, he has a point. Listening today – and most prevalent in the percolating sequenced synthesizer part running throughout – one can almost taste the neon-coloured flavour of a certain Far East city... a foreshadowing of Hong Kong 24 years later?

'Bang' (Albarn, Coxon, James, Rowntree)

A-side single; Released 29 July 1991; UK: 24, US Dance: 40

The follow-up to the big commercial breakthrough that was 'There's No Other Way', was written in record time: fifteen minutes at The Premises rehearsal studio in Hackney, if Alex's recollection is correct. Recorded at Maison Rouge in spring 1991 towards the end of the *Leisure* sessions, the track is another well-produced and tightly-constructed upbeat baggy number.

Boasting Graham's skilful guitar hammer-ons and pull-offs, an inventive Alex bass line, and not to mention another strident Damon chorus, it was expected to follow the previous single into the top ten. When it missed the top 20, there was shock and disappointment for all involved. In reality, the relative failure of 'Bang' was a blessing in disguise. If the song had been a big hit, the band would've likely been forced to continue down this path of frivolous, vacuous pop, thus rendering their subsequent art-punk reinvention on the next single, 'Popscene' an unlikely development. Still, a top-30 chart placing was no disaster and gave momentum to the soon-to-be-released debut album.

Later on, the band all but disowned the track. It was left off their 2000 compilation *Blur: The Best Of*, and was never performed live again after touring for *Leisure* ceased in 1992 (the 1999 Wembley singles-night gig being the only exception). In a 1995 interview with the *NME*, Damon summed up the band's collective feelings when he was asked to name Blur's worst record: ''Bang'! Our worst ever. Just appalling, lyrically and musically. If we ever do a singles compilation, we'll rewrite history to omit it.'

'Slow Down' (Albarn, Coxon, James, Rowntree)

This Stephen Street production is a pretty pop song that Graham transformed into a My Bloody Valentine homage due to its fuzzed-up buzzsaw guitar onslaught. Damon later lamented that this heavy-handed approach ruined the album, but Graham must've felt vindicated when MBV singer/guitarist Kevin Shields later declared himself a fan of the track.

Though a lightweight song lyrically ('All you've got to do/Just you be you'), there are some interesting arrangement touches. At 1:31, it explodes into a double-tempo psychedelic speed trip, replete with Dave's Keith Moon-esque drumming, along with some *Rubber Soul*-era Beatles vocal harmonies shared between Damon and Graham. Several sections feature even more distortion courtesy of Alex's bass (e.g., 0:22-0:29), proving the band were already dabbling with the pop-meets-grunge 'Song 2' sonic formula as early as 1991.

'Repetition' (Albarn, Coxon, James, Rowntree)

Attempted in the studio twice – first by Mike Thorne and then Stephen Street (the latter version being chosen for release) – the sluggishly-paced 'Repetition' was in the band's live set as early as the Seymour days, despite Alex's dislike of the song.

The beeping sound on Graham's bendy guitar hook was achieved after studying a nifty Pete Townshend trick: switching from one pick-up turned up loud, to the other one turned down completely, thus creating a Morse-code effect. Meanwhile, Damon's decidedly nihilistic lyrics border on the Beckettian: 'Try, try, try / All things remain the same / So why try again?' Damon quite literally stumbled upon this realisation one Christmas morning when – aged nineteen – his girlfriend's irate father chased him across a school field. In 1991, Damon told *Q* magazine: 'I was drunk and had wanted to tell her I loved her. There's an enormous emotional reason behind that song, but does the world give a fuck?'

The vocal performance is noteworthy for introducing the compressed midrange megaphone-like sound (in this instance, it *was* a megaphone) favoured so often in his career – heard in tracks by both Blur ('Oily Water', 'Entertain Me') and Gorillaz ('Feel Good Inc', 'Tranz').

'Bad Day' (Albarn, Coxon, James, Rowntree)

For such a sunny-sounding tune, this had a somewhat troubled history. Firstly, Damon wrote it when ill with a streptococcal infection. Then when the band came to record it as a follow-up singe to 'She's So High', producer Steve Power insisted Graham perform Alex's bass parts for him, leaving the bass player miffed. The session was shelved and the band were dejected.

Listening to the spick-and-span Stephen Street-produced album version, you'd never know of its chequered past. The bright 'n' breezy melodica intro gives way to another baggy beat in the unusual time signature of 6/4, with some raucous wah-wah guitar from Graham. Though downbeat in lyrical content, the vocals reveal an attractive melodic flair, with more pretty Beatlesque harmonies in the chorus. There's even a reference to the Syd Barrett song 'Octopus' at 2:45 when Damon sings 'Isn't it good, lost in the wood'.

Ultimately landing as a good-rather-than-great album track, if the song had been called 'Good Day' or 'Rad Day' with the tempo increased a touch, single status might've been restored.

'Sing' (Albarn, Coxon, James, Rowntree)

Often described by critics as *Leisure's* strongest moment, 'Sing' is an early example of the glorious melancholia that would become a defining feature of Damon's best songwriting. The album version was actually a demo recorded at The Roundhouse, Chalk Farm in 1990, after sessions for 'She's So High'.

Performed at gigs in the Seymour days, Alex remembers the song taking shape at Damon's mum Hazel's home art studio when the boys once stayed over. An even earlier demo called 'Sing (To Me)' was recorded during that period, possessing a straight-ahead rock beat, livelier vocal and faster tempo. But this rendition is something else entirely. With a thumping drum pattern akin to the Velvet Underground's 'Waiting for the Man' on valium, a staccato piano chord sequence of Em, A6 and Bm, and Damon's vocal from the pits of despair, 'Sing' was the song that Blur knew made them special – and despite its gloomily-spectral verses, the 'Aaaah sing to me' chorus blasts through the shadows, dripping in sunburst majesty.

Graham – whose reverb-soaked guitar added to the ghostly ambience – claimed that even audience members who disliked Blur would come rushing up to them and say, 'What was that song?'. More importantly, it proved to everyone – fans, critics and label alike – that the band had serious depth and imagination. Though never single material, 'Sing' (with the possible exception of 'There's No Other Way'), is *Leisure*'s best-known piece – its inclusion on the soundtrack to *the* pop culture film of 1996 – *Trainspotting* – giving the anaesthetised lyrics a whole new meaning:

I can't feel
'Cause I'm numb
So what's the worth in all of this?
If the child in your head
If the child is dead

Then there's Coldplay. Chris Martin's group seem to enjoy endlessly recycling elements of 'Sing' in their own work: 'Politik', 'Lost!' and 'Hymn for the Weekend', to name a few examples.

'There's No Other Way' (Albarn, Coxon, James, Rowntree)

Single A-side. Released 15 April 1991. UK: 7, US: 82, US Alt-rock: 5

Here comes success. This track is historically significant in the Blur timeline for not only being their first bona fide UK hit single, but also for being the first time they'd work with the man who became integral to so many of their future recordings: ex-The Smiths producer, Stephen Street.

With the Steve Lovell-produced sessions for the proposed second single 'Bad Day' aborted, Blur's label Food were now looking for someone else to record the band's next effort and get things back on track. As luck would have it, Street had seen 'She's So High' reviewed on the TV show *Juke Box Jury* and liked what he heard. His management got in touch with Food, and after a meeting with the boys, he was hired to produce the next single.

Work began at Maison Rouge in the first week of January 1991. Originally intended for the B-side of another song they were recording, 'Come Together', There's No Other Way' was written quickly, and the band regarded it as a throwaway. However, as soon as they started working on the rhythm track – a looped baggy breakbeat mixed with Dave's live drums and an effervescent Alex bass line – the recording was sounding like a hit. A little-known fact which Street recently revealed, is that the drum loop was sampled from the Run DMC track 'What's It All About'. This had in turn been taken from The Stone Roses' 'Fools Gold', so in that regard, 'There's No Other Way' features a second-generation sample of The Stone Roses!

Another slam dunk was Graham's capo-aided guitar lick in E. Bluesy, but busy, slippery yet sturdy, it's one of his best. Meanwhile, the liquid riff during the post-breakdown chorus – in which the guitar and bass play in unison – is another seductive touch. From Graham's own admission, it was heavily influenced by US funk band The Meters (Refer to their 1969 instrumental 'Sissy Strut').

Though lyrically inert, in this context, it's strangely fitting, giving the track a certain detached swagger. Damon again sounds a little like Syd Barrett, with Pink Floyd's 'See Emily Play' being a possible influence on the chorus. Add to this some high, smiling vocal harmonies and a 1960s psychedelic backwards guitar solo, and the band were in business: 'There's no other way, there's no other way / All that you can do is watch them play.'

Entering the UK singles chart at number 20 and gradually climbing to a peak of number 8, the song also did well in the US – hitting number 5 on the Modern Rock chart and 82 on the Billboard Hot 100. Legend has it that during a 1991 radio interview when Kurt Cobain was asked about his favourite recent tracks to come out of England, he replied by singing the intro guitar riff to 'There's No Other Way'. What isn't in any doubt (and despite the very of-its-time Stone Roses vs Charlatans 'baggy' pop sound), is that the track almost single-handedly propelled its parent album *Leisure* into the top 10, thus establishing Blur as a major force on the indie rock scene.

'Fool' (Albarn, Coxon, James, Rowntree)

Depicted by Alex as 'Damon trying to be Morrissey', 'Fool' is a jangle-pop love song not unlike 'Slow Down', with sappy pleading lyrics causing the frontman to come off like an indie-rock George McFly. Indeed, the line 'Couldn't you try to forgive a fool' sounds almost like an excerpt from 'Earth Angel' – the song Marty McFly performed onstage in *Back to the Future*.

Toughened up by another My Bloody Valentine guitar onslaught from Graham, the middle section at 1:30 brings a bizarre tempo change: an obvious attempt to copy MBV's 'Nothing Much To Lose'. Graham even plays (uncredited) drums in this section, presumably to show Dave the part.

Mike Thorne produced the track (Wire, Soft Cell). He was brought in to oversee some of the more esoteric tracks while Stephen Street was in New York recording the final Psychedelic Furs album *World Outside*.

'Come Together' (Albarn, Coxon, James, Rowntree)

Recorded with Stephen Street in the same sessions as 'There's No Other Way', 'Come Together' – in Graham's estimation – suffered from 'a lack of abandon'. Listening to the raucous live rendition from the Kilburn National in 1991, you can see his point. Despite this assertion, it's one of the few *Leisure* tracks where the band – particularly Dave – are given room to let loose.

Despite the derivative nature of the swirling E to G verse sequence, producer Street was impressed with Graham's quick bending of the minor-to-major chord notes, and Alex's bass line is typically fruity. Unfortunately, the vocal melody is neither memorable nor particularly tuneful, and naming the song after a Beatles classic is surely asking for unfavourable comparisons with the Liverpudlian legends.

'High Cool' (Albarn, Coxon, James, Rowntree)

Named after an air conditioning unit setting at the Premises rehearsal space, this is a fun-'n'-funky Stephen Street production, and *Leisure*'s last-recorded track. Perhaps spurred on by the album almost being complete, Damon's lyrics and vocal delivery are confident and purposeful, verging on the combative: 'If you come here / Which you sometimes do / Don't think that I really want you to.'

Combined with a 12-bar-blues chord sequence, these lines make 'High Cool' come across like an early-1990s indie-pop version of Dave Bartholomew's 'I Hear You Knocking'.

Elsewhere, the pauses after the chorus – with their compressed vintage-sounding drum fills and Alex's Prince-like bass line (which was modelled on 'Mountains' from the *Parade* album) add to a pleasing if undemanding listen.

'Birthday' (Albarn, Coxon, James, Rowntree)

Damon wrote 'Birthday' at the piano after a heavy night out – he woke up in a prison cell next to a Gurkha. The song made quite an impression on those in the band's orbit. When Graham first heard Damon's demo, he thought it was 'one of the greatest little songs' he'd ever heard. Similarly, Blur's publisher Mike Smith also attested it was this song that suggested the band had some phenomenal writing talent.

It's a beautifully sincere rumination on the more melancholic realities of one's own anniversary, at odds with more celebratory offerings from the likes of The Beatles, Stevie Wonder or Altered Images:

It's my birthday, no one here day
Very strange day, I think of you day
Go outside day, sit in park day
Watch the sky day, what a pathetic day
I don't like this day, it makes me feel so small

Produced by Mike Thorne, the song's vocal section lays on a gentle psychedelic bed of piano, backwards guitar, bass, tambourine and harmony backing vocals. Damon was sceptical of the grungy instrumental section that enters at 2:44, and it might've had greater impact if they'd added jovial samples of laughter, bottles clinking and people singing 'Happy Birthday'. This could've demonstrated in sarcastically sinister fashion, the dichotomy of the protagonist's situation against the standard prosaic take on birthdays most of us succumb to.

'Wear Me Down' (Albarn, Coxon, James, Rowntree)

The album's final track is also its most *in-your-face* old-school rock moment, and is another Mike Thorne production. Opening with a hyper-distorted Hendrixian guitar riff from Graham, the rhythm section crash in soon afterwards, creating a heavy Black Sabbath-esque sonic brew. In contrast to this, Damon's rather insipid vocal is delivered in hushed tones – so much so, you can barely recognise it's him, and the use of a de-esser (an effect that lessens harsh 'S' consonant sounds) on his vocal adds to this notion (his super sibilant 's' being a defining vocal characteristic). The lyrics follow suit, portraying a man who is frazzled, battered and defeated: 'You wear me down / My defences are gone now / And I can't fight.'

It works, though, and the 1960s-pop style chorus with added harmonies is a welcome respite from the soup-thick verses, which happen to bear a certain chordal similarity to Nirvana's 'In Bloom'.

But the man of the match here turns out to be Dave. His increasingly dexterous drum fills – accompanied by an abundance of loud, earsplitting cymbal crashes – threaten to explode towards the end. Credit should therefore be given to Mike Thorne for allowing this to happen – he was even adamant that the song be released as a single, proof that he was a producer with refreshingly non-mainstream ideals.

Contemporary Tracks

'I Know' (Albarn, Coxon, James, Rowntree)

Double A-side single b/w 'She's So High'

The first of many clashes in Blur's battle-strewn career was against their own record label, with Food Records favouring 'I Know' for the first single over the band's choice of 'She's So High'. Although the boys prevailed, it's easy to see why the label were keen on this track, and it was eventually included on the US version of *Leisure* in place of 'Sing'. Not only was it the more upbeat, less introspective option of the two, it possessed the most voguish qualities.

Surfing the coattails of the Stones Roses-and-Charlatans-fronted UK indie dance craze, 'I Know' was a transparent attempt to join the gang. Graham – whose John Squire-aping, wah-wah guitar riffing is the guiltiest homage (Squire was guitarist for The Stone Roses) – admitted that they used the style as a stepping stone to get noticed. In that respect, they succeeded.

Recorded with Steve Lovell in the same sessions as the debut single, this faintly psychedelic alt-dance offering is a likeable yet trite affair, ultimately betraying the band's potential for originality.

'Down' (Albarn, Coxon, James, Rowntree)

B-side of 'She's So High'

During Blur's 1999 B-sides gig at the Electric Ballroom in Camden, Damon announced 'Down' as a song from when 'we thought we were Spaceman 3'. Though not an entirely accurate statement, the song does possess a certain strung-out languor favoured by Spacemen 3 members Peter Kember and Jason Pierce, particularly in the drone-like chorus that Damon and Graham sing in an almost monotone fashion.

Elsewhere, Graham again lives out his My Bloody Valentine guitar fantasies, creating a thick-'n'-sludgy tone that he admitted was the result of a then-unrefined playing style. Thoughts on this self-produced track were muted – Alex reckoned the song was 'all over the place', while Andy Ross at Food Records felt it 'belonged to another incarnation'.

'Inertia' (Albarn, Coxon, James, Rowntree)

B-side of 'There's No Other Way'

Like so many of Blur's self-produced B-sides and demos of this period, 'Inertia' was recorded at Matrix Studios – originally on Little Russell Street, before being relocated to Parsons Green in 2000. Recorded in 1991, this song was noteworthy for being Blur's first session with engineer John Smith, who was to work with the band on every album and B-side up to and including *13*. Not only was he a supportive and sympathetic presence, but he was also responsible for so many of the sounds and sonics of future recordings.

A languidly-elegant modern blues, the song opens with guitar arpeggios over a chord sequence of G6, F#7sus4 (both with an open 1st string) and E, not unlike a reverse rendition of 'This Is a Low'. Damon's vocal is gentle and soothing, possessing more subtlety and emotion than many of his *Leisure* performances. The lyrics are an astute rumination on the mindless treadmill that forever thrusts society forward, and perhaps is even a statement on Damon's own place in pop culture:

Fear of being left behind, can take you over
Slowly you will choke, or maybe it's just a joke
I'm not sure, are you?

The band were all extremely fond of this track and were subsequently regretful of its absence – along with several other B-sides – from *Leisure.* It would've certainly made sense as a bridge between the arty, esoteric Seymour and *Modern Life Is Rubbish*. Also, its inclusion may have given the finished *Leisure* more breadth and depth, slotting in nicely as a replacement for 'Repetition'.

'Mr Briggs' (Albarn, Coxon, James, Rowntree)

B-side of 'There's No Other Way'

Another song the band wished they'd included on *Leisure* was this self-produced track recorded towards the end of 1990. Indeed it was Damon's first attempt at a character-based song, and thus would've given listeners an embryonic glimpse into the slowly-developing world of 'Colin Zeal' and 'Tracy Jacks'.

Based on a Liverpudlian that Damon encountered while occupying a Greenwich bedsit in 1990, the song is a Syd Barrett-type character study, with the humorously-humdrum lyrics echoing the erstwhile Pink Floyd leader's mundane whimsy:

He has a three-bar heater but it don't keep him warm
If he bought another, then he'd have one more

The instrumentation showcases Dave's Ringo-esque 'A Day in the Life' drum fills, while the guitars offer a good summary of Graham's range at the time, veering from nimble-fingered bluesy riffs (0:08 and 0:26), to reverb-drenched My Bloody Valentine-esque wailing (1:30-1:50).

'I'm All Over' (Albarn, Coxon, James, Rowntree)

B-side of 'There's No Other Way'

This jumpy song contains a lyric rife with detachment and isolation, totally at odds with it's energetic musical accompaniment: 'I always knew there would be no one nowhere / Who was anything like me.'

Hardly a memorable moment in Blur's vast canon, perhaps its most distinguishing feature is Dave's jerky snare-heavy drum pattern: pilfered allegedly from Betty Boo's 'Where Are You Baby?' at Graham's instruction. Despite this, the guitarist was not a fan, calling it 'a ridiculous song with a terrible synthetic drumbeat'.

'Won't Do It' (Albarn, Coxon, James, Rowntree)

B-side of 'There's No Other Way'

A remnant from the Seymour days, the idea behind this frantic thrash was for the band to produce a chorus written around one single note. Ironically, it's the song's downfall – there's simply not enough in the way of melody to make it distinct or compelling, despite the presence of such impressive punkish vigour. Still, the half-speed middle section (1:31 to 2:55) does boast a welcome supersonic swirl of atonal guitars, groovy bass and funky rhythms, causing a dizzying disorientation that gradually speeds up to climax into the final chorus.

'Day Upon Day' (Albarn, Coxon, James, Rowntree)

B-side of 'There's No Other Way'

Presenting as a slightly catchier twin sibling to 'Won't Do It', 'Day Upon Day' was the first live track that Blur released. Their then-tour-manager Drac recorded the song from the desk at Moles nightclub in Bath during the autumn-1990 tour promoting 'She's So High'.

Creeping up like the dawn, Graham's gently-strummed G chord gradually increases in volume until the rest of the band burst in, with Dave playing a particular lively drum pattern: all open hi-hats and double snare hits. The hooky, repetitive chorus in which Damon repeats the title over and over, is bolstered via Graham's spiky Beatles 'Taxman' chords, creating an affecting on/off/on/off rhythmic pulse.

The song was often performed as an encore in the 1990-1992 period, and, for Damon, seems to be associated with personal injury. On this particular recording, he was singing with a broken nose after being accidentally smacked in the face earlier in the set with the machine heads on the bass as Alex span around wildly.

More notoriously, it was during a 1992 Glastonbury festival performance of 'Day Upon Day' that Damon jumped against a stack of PA speakers, causing them to tumble down and land agonisingly on the back of his ankles as he walked away. This and his subsequent howls of pain as he limped off stage, are captured in (in)glorious technicolor in the documentary *Starshaped*.

'Explain' (Albarn, Coxon, James, Rowntree)

B-side of 'Bang'

Talking of the *Starshaped* film, those who have seen it will be familiar with this rollicking number. In one of the movie's more comical scenes – aboard the tour bus late one night – Blur's road manager Ifan Thomas pokes his head through the curtain of his bunk to tell the band and whoever else is present, to go to bed. Unfortunately for him, they are not compos mentis, especially Dave, who is flailing about hopelessly while 'Explain' blares out of the stereo system.

Regardless of the state the band were in, they seem to be genuinely enjoying rocking out to this track, with Damon audibly singing at the top of his lungs. It's highly doubtful you'd see them enjoying a drunken sing-along to 'Bang' in quite the same fashion. This leads one to pose the question: would 'Explain' have been a better single choice over its eventual A-side? Sure, it's a pretty lightweight lyric, but then so were many of Damon's at the time, and the boy-with-girl-trouble scenario might've resonated with a wider cross-section of their then-youthful audience.

Graham's intro guitar lick is simple yet direct, and the rhythm section is funky and loose. The inclusion of quasi-barroom piano in the main arrangement provides a certain suburban Americana flavour and mildly resembles EMF's megahit 'Unbelievable', released just a few months before. At 1:46, there's even a full band wig out section not dissimilar to 'Wear Me Down', which would've appealed to the rock kids.

Recorded with Stephen Street in May 1991 during the sessions that produced 'High Cool', 'Explain' can nevertheless be expounded as a source of the boys' affection for years afterwards, being a song written during carefree pre-record-deal nights at the Beat Factory.

'Luminous' (Albarn, Coxon, James, Rowntree)

B-side of 'Bang'

'Luminous' was cut with John Smith at Matrix during the same sessions that produced 'Inertia'. It was another one of those B-sides that the band would love to have snuck onto *Leisure*, though it did appear on Japanese copies. Damon was extremely fond of the song, praising its 'really lovely feel'.

Depending on your point of view, this seductively-atmospheric affair was achieved despite or due to the band being drunk and stoned. Damon's lyrics here exude a poetic ambiguity that can be traced through to future cuts such as 'This Is a Low' and '1992', while the melody line sits halfway between future efforts 'Bone Bag' and 'Far Out': 'No substitute for the girl of dreams / She never knew who you were.'

Graham's woozy guitar chords add to the gently-psychedelic ambience, employing the Kevin Shields (My Bloody Valentine guitarist) technique of strumming while slowly moving the guitar's tremolo arm.

Blur attempted to include 'Luminous' in their live shows around this period, but Graham reportedly struggled to sing and play it simultaneously, with the often hapless results causing him embarrassment.

'Berserk' (Albarn, Coxon, James, Rowntree)

B-side of 'Bang'

The first instrumental that Blur released, the almost seven-minute-long 'Berserk', is an unsettling freak-out devised by Graham, employing the use of backwards guitar and two drum loops, one of which he performs and then is reversed. Damon's long-drawn-out Hammond organ chords add to the droning cacophony and prompt the conclusion that 'Berserk' is a wordless demented twin of The Beatles' 'Blue Jay Way'.

Being easily the strangest track that Blur recorded in this period, Food boss Andy Ross was far from impressed, believing that it wasn't worth the effort. He has a point, but at the least, its title hit the mark!

'Uncle Love' (Albarn, Coxon, James, Rowntree)

B-side of 'Bang'

Had this track been re-recorded – or at least remixed by Stephen Street – it would've surely been a contender for inclusion on *Leisure.* An early attempt at the Syd Barrett/David Bowie/Ray Davies- style character studies that came to fruition on the next album, 'Uncle Love' is a charmingly peppy and tightly-constructed track that would've made a great substitute for 'Fool' or 'Come Together'.

Damon's semi-cockney delivery makes one think of David Bowie's 'Uncle Arthur' from his self-titled debut but instead sung by Syd Barrett, and with a less succinct story arc. Graham described his sprightly guitar work as being 'like J Mascis on Prozac', while his eight-note clean-tone phrase during the 'Uncle Love's gonna get you' section is a dreamy delight, adding a twinkle to the protagonist's eye.

Written and recorded one Thursday evening between watching *Top of the Pops* and going out to nightclub Syndrome, 'Uncle Love' captures Blur in jubilant form, no doubt pumped up by the recent success of 'There's No Other Way'.

'I Love Her' (Albarn, Coxon, James, Rowntree)

Fan club single CD#2. Released October 1997

Recorded in 1991 at Diarama Studios in Great Portland Street, this song never made it past the demo stage. Based on looped drums, guitar and bass, this vaguely funky Deee-Lite-esque track bares a slight lyric resemblance to 'She's So High': 'She don't care if I live or die / That is why I love her.'

Meanwhile, the main E7 to A7 guitar riff sounds a lot like a prototype for 'Eat My Goal' – the 1996 Coca-Cola-endorsed track by fellow north-Essex band Collapsed Lung.

Blur eventually performed a faster, punkier version during their 1999 B-sides gig, where they dedicated it to Stephen Street. A recording of this arguably-inferior version – featuring a harder Damon vocal – was cut in late 1991 (around the same time 'Popscene' was demoed) and was unearthed for the *21* box set in 2012.

'Close' (Albarn, Coxon, James, Rowntree)

Fan club single CD#3. Released November 1998.

Produced by Stephen Street during the 1991 *Leisure* sessions, 'Close' had originally been attempted with Steve Lovell in late-1990, but was scrapped alongside his version of 'Bad Day'. Another Seymour-era song, an early rendition of 'Close' can be heard in footage of their 1989 gig at The Square in Harlow.

Fading in with a promising, screechy one-chord intro that's not unlike 'Villa Rosie', the track settles into familiar 1991 Blur territory at 0:10 – bluesy agile riffing from Graham, a bouncy rhythm track from Alex and Dave, while Damon sings in an icily-detached manner. The instrumental section at 2:09 boasts Graham's quirky, off-kilter vibrato guitar textures, which hint at the direction his playing would soon take.

Catchy and commercial, yet ultimately froth, Food likely commissioned it for those very reasons, in the hope that Street's finished version would have single potential. It was *close*, but no cigar.

Modern Life Is Rubbish (1993)

Personnel:
Damon Albarn: lead vocals, keyboards, piano
Graham Coxon: guitars, backing vocals, percussion, Black and Decker drill
Alex James: bass
Dave Rowntree: drums, percussion
Stephen Street: drumbox, handclaps, Casio S1000, typewriter bell
The Kick Horns: brass
Kate St John: oboe, cor anglais, saxophone
The Duke String Quartet: strings
Miriam Stockley and Mae McKenna: backing vocals on 'For Tomorrow'
Recorded: October 1991-March 1993 at Matrix and Maison Rouge studios
Producers: Stephen Street, Steve Lovell, John Smith, Blur
Release dates: UK: 10 May 1993, US: 16 November 1993
Label: Food/Parlophone (UK), SBK (US)
Chart Placings: UK: 15, US: did not chart

Following the near-gold-disc success of *Leisure,* Food Records sent Blur straight back into Matrix studios in October 1991 to record demos for a planned second album. Optimistically and somewhat naively, the guys had hoped for a Spring 1992 release date for the new LP, drawing up a rough track list which included 'Oily Water', 'Mace', 'Badgeman Brown', 'Popscene', 'Resigned', 'Garden Central', 'Hanging Over', 'Into Another', 'Peach', 'Bone Bag', 'Never Clever', 'Coping', 'My Ark' and 'Pressure on Julian'. As a result of their commercially-satisfied label temporarily relaxing scrutiny, these new tracks were lugubriously introspective and psychedelic in tone, closer representing the sound Blur had wished to purvey on their debut.

Nevertheless, this proposed album never saw the light of day, due to two main factors. Firstly, when Food boss Dave Balfe finally heard the new recordings, he hated most of them, arguing that the band should be aiming to take over the world, not settle for middling indie status. Secondly, and perhaps more significant, was the failure of the April 1992 single 'Popscene'. Stalling at 32 on the UK chart, it prompted Food to scrap plans for the follow-up single 'Never Clever', and instead ordered Blur back to the drawing board.

A difficult and troubling year ensued, with the band sacking manager Mike Collins for financial mishandling (Chris Morrison was subsequently hired, who they had originally rejected), and a miserable April-June US tour led the guys to the edge of their wits, and to blows with each other. They then returned home, only to learn that their domestic popularity had plummeted, with hot new band Suede (led by Elastica singer Justine Frischmann's ex Brett Anderson) breaking through and lapping up all the UK press plaudits.

Meanwhile, new Blur recordings with XTC's Andy Partridge at The Church Studios in Crouch End were deemed unsatisfactory by the band, despite it being very much their idea to hire him in the first place. Graham Coxon explained in *3862 Days*:

> I was a big XTC fan. I liked the idea of Andy Partridge producing us. The trouble was that it ended up sounding like Andy Partridge's music at that time. You might want to sound like The Eagles, but not Don Henley, you know.

Damon has also stated that the sessions possessed a strange vibe due to Partridge continually saying 'Don't make the mistakes I made', reckoning that he didn't really know how to be a producer.

Partridge himself recalled that Graham was usually drunk during the sessions, and that Damon was preoccupied with his girlfriend Justine, repeatedly arriving late to the studio. Whatever the truth was, and despite Food's Andy Ross arguing that the tracks 'sounded great', these recordings of 'Sunday Sunday', 'Coping', and '7 Days' (with a samba rendition of 'Starshaped' abandoned) were shelved at the band's own insistence, not even permitting Food to issue them as B-sides. The now-exasperated record label were on the brink of dropping the penniless and desperate Blur.

Luckily, a chance meeting between Graham and Stephen Street took place at the Marquee during a Cranberries gig on 1 October 1992, prompting the guys to fight tooth-and-nail with Food to reinstate the producer of their biggest-selling single to date. The band were vindicated when Street eventually returned to the fold – happily and fruitfully recording together at Maison Rouge solidly between November 1992 and March 1993.

Though a few more serious challenges and hiccups arose along the way (see 'For Tomorrow' and 'Chemical World'), Blur's second album was eventually released in May 1993. Replacing its working title of *Britain Versus America*, the record was ultimately christened *Modern Life Is Rubbish*, after a piece of stencilled graffiti painted along West London's Bayswater Road. Gone were the baggy indie-dance rhythms and vacuous lyrics of *Leisure* – in their place, sharply-observational songwriting with taut, intricately-constructed arrangements in the quintessentially classic British pop mould of The Kinks, The Beatles and XTC.

Hitting the UK top 20 and selling around 40,000 copies initially, the album just about kept the band's head above water commercially. More importantly, it marked an artistic turning point for Blur, laying the groundwork for the epochal third album *Parklife*, and putting them on a trajectory towards becoming one of Britain's biggest and most critically-acclaimed 1990s bands.

'For Tomorrow' (Albarn, Coxon, James, Rowntree)

A-side single. Released 19 April 1993. UK: 28

Though it was actually the penultimate song recorded for *Modern Life Is Rubbish*, 'For Tomorrow' was truly the beginning of a rebirth for Blur.

In December 1992, the band had just finished recording their proposed second album. Rejecting the group's twelve-track submission for a *Leisure* follow-up, Food boss Dave Balfe told Damon that it lacked a single, and that if they wanted this new album to be released at all, they must come up with one, and quick. You can imagine the group's frustration and disappointment after toiling for well over a year on this new LP. Understandably, that Christmas, Damon returned to his parent's house in Colchester feeling miserable, going out on Christmas Eve to drown his sorrows. Rising extremely early the next morning, hungover, he wrote 'For Tomorrow' in the family kitchen, to the chagrin of his rudely awoken father Keith. But it was worth the trouble.

Convening back in London after the new year, the label were impressed with Damon's home demo, hearing the commercial potential in the 'La la la la la / Holding on for tomorrow' chorus hook. The rest of the band were similarly enthused and were duly sent back into Maison Rouge with Stephen Street to record the track.

The shimmering backwards reverb that preceded Graham's acoustic guitar intro ushered in a new dawn of sophisticated and sweeping pop, a million miles from the faceless indie thrashing often found on *Leisure.* Perhaps one of the most significant aspects to strike on the first listen is the chord structure's sheer complexity when measured against previous Blur releases. There are no fewer than twelve different chords in the opening verse and chorus, and it never really settles in any key for too long. After all this harmonic fluidity, the chorus lands on and stays in the relative minor of C: A minor.

Lyrically, Damon paints a picture of London life moving forth at dizzying speed, full of 20th-century boys and girls doing their utmost to keep up the pace, clinging to each other and singing through the fear and uncertainty. Incidentally, the opening line was influenced by a 1964 track called 'He's a 20th Century Englishman', written and recorded by singer Alan Klein. It was on an album called *Well At Least It's British,* which Damon picked up in a charity shop. Despite its obscurity, the record became a big source of songwriting inspiration for him in this period and - listening to Klein's song, it also sounds like it could've been an influence on David Bowie's 1967 debut album.

Speaking of Bowie, his presence rains down heavily upon the style and arrangement of 'For Tomorrow', with Damon affecting a high-baritone cockney vocal straight from the *Hunky Dory* era, and the melodramatic but brilliant string arrangement is in the same mould as the *Hunky Dory* epics 'Life on Mars', 'Changes' and 'Quicksand'. Elsewhere, Stephen Street instructed backing vocalists Miriam Stockley and Mae McKenna to sing like The Thunderthighs – the backing vocal group Bowie had helped produce on the 1972 Lou Reed LP *Transformer*.

The finished product blended seamlessly, and in Street's correct estimation, 'For Tomorrow' was the best thing the guys had yet committed to tape. Released as Blur's big comeback single after the disappointing performance of 'Popscene' the previous year, 'For Tomorrow' was probably a little too esoteric to be a big hit. Falling short of expectations, it hit number 28 in the UK, though its parent album came in at number 15 a few weeks later, easing concerns. Blur were still alive and 'holding on for tomorrow' – Just about.

'Advert' (Albarn, Coxon, James, Rowntree)
Picking up stylistically from where 'Popscene' left off, 'Advert' is the album's punkiest and most aggressive track. Damon sampled the inane opening proclamation 'Food processors are great!' from the shopping channel, using a Casio SK1 keyboard. Then, just before the full band crashes in, there's a tinkly toy-town intro with programmed drums, plinky-plonky piano, and Graham's wobbly one-note guitar motif, achieved by manually detuning the struck string up and down. Fans of the late-1990s British comedy program *The Adam & Joe Show* may hear the possible influence this section had on that show's theme tune.

The verses' A to G guitar vamp thrashes away like an energetic take on the classic Ray Davies/Kinks riff heard on 'Tired of Waiting for You' or 'Where Have All the Good Times Gone' – a device Blur often employed in the period between 1993 and 1995 (e.g. 'Bank Holiday', 'Dan Abnormal' etc.).

Lyrically, Damon paints a picture of sick and tired commuters travelling home on the London underground – the advertising staring back from the tube walls seducing them with the promise of a holiday in paradise:

> You need a holiday, somewhere in the sun
> With all the people who are waiting
> There never seems to be one

It's not quite clear if he's sympathetic to the protagonist's situation or not, but the sarcastic yelped delivery of the line 'Say something, say something else' speaks volumes about his attitude towards the adverts themselves.

'Colin Zeal' (Albarn, Coxon, James, Rowntree)
This first of Damon's Kinks-esque character studies to appear on a Blur album was written during a 1991 US tour and performed as early as February 1992. Featuring a verse vocal melody and chord sequence liberally borrowed from 'Sleeping Gas' by The Teardrop Explodes, the song details attributes of an enthusiastic and energetic workaday type fellow, cut from the same cloth as The Kinks' 'Mr Pleasant' or 'Plastic Man'.

The message here is that despite all the 'bombast' and affability on the surface, underneath, he's nothing but a soulless 'retard', obsessed with smart clothes and being successful. Though described by Damon as a 'nasty little' man, Damon could just as well be having a dig at himself here, uniting his own compulsion towards fame and success with his more cerebral, self-critical tendencies.

Only the second track to be recorded after re-uniting with producer Stephen Street, 'Colin Zeal' is a smartly-arranged piece, with some particularly nifty and nimble bass-playing from Alex. Elsewhere, Graham is in typically-diverse form, deploying rhythmically tight chordal work in the verses (with some mysterious lead wah-wah phrases over the top), while he goes full-on stadium-rock in the instrumental middle. There's also a curious two-bar atonal section at 2:04, featuring Stephen Street on the Casio S1000. This is a direct imitation of a passage from David Bowie's cover of Pink Floyd's 'See Emily Play' (0:49-0:53) on his 1973 *Pin Ups* LP.

'Pressure on Julian' (Albarn, Coxon, James, Rowntree)

The eerily hypnotic opening guitar intro is indicative of the overall mood. Creeping, psychedelic, and slightly sinister, the track was originally written around September 1991 and demoed the following January at Matrix.

Though lyrically obtuse, the words do somehow conjure vague images of a poor young lad being tormented from above – *Truman Show*-style – by an array of deliriously-demented bystanders and overlords:

> Swimming in yellow pissy water
> Sand getting in between their ears
> No blood in head in this bloody weather
> Irate people with yellow tongues
>
> We planned it all this way
> Pressure on Julian

The 'magical transit children' mentioned in the first verse was a piece of graffiti Damon spotted during a *Melody Maker* photo shoot near St Pancras. Another Teardrop Explodes reference, the song's protagonist is named after that band's singer and ex-bandmate of Food Records boss Dave Balfe: Julian Cope. In this period, Damon was quite inclined to wind up Balfe with musical and lyrical references to Cope, as it used to 'drive him bananas'.

The track is more interesting sonically than compositionally, though the chorus chord changes are a little odd. It was Graham who played the biggest part in creating some of the more unusual auditory textures – instructing engineer John Smith to mess wildly with the EQ setting on the big crashing guitar chord at 2:43; even more perversely, *playing* a Black and Decker power drill at the end. In relation to the guitarist's unruly characteristic, Damon rather patronisingly claimed that 'The trick with Graham, is to give him the illusion that he's making a racket'. But Damon's grip on this aspect of Graham's input was to become weaker as Blur's career developed.

'Starshaped' (Albarn, Coxon, James, Rowntree)

In late 1992, Blur were at Maison Rouge with Stephen Street, putting the finishing touches on their as-yet-untitled second album. Or so they thought. As Alex was toiling with the bass line for 'Starshaped' (the planned final track to be recorded), Food's Dave Balfe came in to tell them they were making a huge mistake, and on the evidence of this track, they were collectively soon for the chopping block.

Ironically, this rousing power-pop sparkler of a tune was, up to that point, one of the best things the band had attempted, and was assumed to be a future single. Bursting with clever ideas and joyous hooks, 'Starshaped' was a showcase for Damon's ever-improving and complex songwriting. Like many of his songs in this period, chords fly all over the place, keys change from verse (A Major) to chorus (E Major), and the listener is bombarded with rich lyrical imagery. The title itself – which Damon came across in the Kurt Vonnegut novel *Breakfast of Champions* – refers to a state of blissful ignorance.

Graham played a pivotal part in the arrangement, devising a slamming chordal intro, the full-on arena rock middle section from 1:53 to 2:11, and the drone-like one-chord outro. Here, he also plays the 'anti cat and dog' Moog tone, thus called because it slowly rises out of human hearing range into that perceivable by dogs.

Pleasingly – and for the first time on a Blur album – there's also a woodwind and brass passage (1:38-1:53) performed by Kate St John, who, like Dave Balfe, had performed with The Teardrop Explodes in the early-1980s. The oboe and cor anglais counterpoint gives the section a wonderful old-English flavour, embellished with Damon and Graham's Cockney Rebel-esque 'ooh la la la' harmonies.

Incredulously, earlier that year, when Blur first tackled an arrangement for the song with XTC's Andy Partridge, he insisted they try it in a samba style. The band hated it and promptly scrapped it.

'Blue Jeans' (Albarn, Coxon, James, Rowntree)

At the time, this delicate, gentle gem was one of the most autobiographical pieces that Damon had written. Stephen Street told *Uncut* in 2009: 'He was still writing a lot about characters at this point, rather than himself, although 'Blue Jeans' was actually him, talking about a day shopping in Portobello Road. I do wonder if it's about Justine (Frischmann) too. It conjured up a lazy day with nothing, in particular, to do in Damon's life in west London.'

The lyric and vocal convey a sense of tender warmth, while the final line, 'You know it's to be with you,' offers a glimpse of sadness, professing that all he really wants to do is be with the one he loves. But this is not how his life was to pan out:

> And don't think I'm walking out of this
> She don't mind
> Whatever I say, whatever I say
> I don't really wanna change a thing
> I wanna stay this way forever

The track opens with Dave's looped drum pattern played on a refreshingly natural-sounding kit. A satisfying serendipitous effect occurs here too, whereby the arrangement's beat emphasis changes as the song progresses, due to the verses' final section having only four bars to them, whereas the drum loop is eight bars long.

Like the colour of the clothing in its title, 'Blue Jeans' possesses earthy, pastel tones, with Damon's melodica and piano to the fore, for once subduing Graham into a sympathetic supporting role. The rhythmically tight verse guitar volume-pedal parts caused Graham some difficulty, him later saying it was difficult to get right. But it was worth the effort, and accompanied the melodica perfectly – the two instruments together creating the effect of an accordion quickly breathing in and out. Brian Wilson would be proud.

Immaculately produced by Stephen Street concurrently with the vastly differing selections 'Colin Zeal' and 'Advert', 'Blue Jeans' should also be a source of affection for Alex, who recorded his bass part 'completed pissed' after spending the day drinking with band accountant Julian Headley. Hopefully, the rather lovely end result helped decrease some of the pressure on the band's employed bookkeeper.

'Chemical World' (Albarn, Coxon, James, Rowntree)

A-side single. Released 28 June 1993. UK:28, US: Alt:27

Instead of giving the boys a pat on the back for pulling the semi-miraculous 'For Tomorrow' out of the bag, Blur's US record label SBK voiced concern that there was still no American hit on *Modern Life Is Rubbish*. Now close to the end of his tether, Damon went away and angrily wrote 'Chemical World' (sarcastically dubbed 'Americana'), rounding up the troops for a demo session at Roundhouse Studios in Chalk Farm where, nearly three years before, the band had tracked 'Sing' in much less hurried circumstances.

To appease SBK, the final recording – helmed by the ever-dependable Stephen Street in February 1993 – was designed to sound sonically powerful; and they pulled it off. Opening with the band on swaggering full throttle, the track is identifiable for its big roomy drums and crunchy aggressive guitar chords, though the underpinning acoustic strums add a light texture that thwarts any heavy-handedness. Remarkably, in the end, the American label eventually used the softer, more puny Roundhouse demo on the US release, proving themselves to be a hypocritically irrelevant nuisance. Still, for all the frustration and anguish the seemingly never-ending demands to improve the album caused, in the end, they did Blur a favour because begrudgingly it *was* an improved article, and they'd survived another mettle test with more priceless business savvy in their collective armoury.

Thankfully, it's one of the record's strongest tracks, building on the anthemic strands developed in 'For Tomorrow', and staying in line with that song's lyrical thread. Evidently in despair of the ever-increasing industrialisation and cheapness of modern life, 'Chemical World' paints a picture of an inner-city checkout girl fleeing her life in the cold lonely city, for a restorative break in the countryside, only to find that she now has insufficient funds to pay her rent. Meanwhile, the line 'These townies, they never speak to you' exposes itself as a token of Damon's bile, presumably stemming from his teenage years growing up in Colchester.

To offset some of the deliberately dense sonics, the chorus offers some affecting Beatlesque harmonies on the 'ooohs' and the 'yes, yes', and Grahams ultra-flanged guitar-picking in the pre-verse breakdowns is an exquisite touch.

Soon after this, the band rather incredulously had to record the song yet again – this time with ex-Madness producers Clive Langer and Alan Winstanley – for a cut that ended up as an alternative offering on one of the single issues. No matter, though, because it was the Stephen Street-produced version that ended up on the album and was released as a single A-Side in June 1993, landing in the exact same chart position as 'For Tomorrow'. Blur were now – commercially speaking – treading water, but at the same time were artistically and culturally gearing up for one almighty splash.

'Intermission' (Albarn, Coxon, James, Rowntree)

A Kurt Weill-influenced instrumental, 'Intermission' was originally performed at early Seymour gigs and was known simply as 'The Intro' – opening and closing live sets respectively alongside its twin piece 'The Outro' (aka 'Commercial Break'). It was during this opening number that Graham recalled how Damon would often throw up due to the combination of overexertion and drinking too much before a show.

Opening with Damon's jaunty menacing piano motif (circling from the key of E minor to Eb major and back again) and punctuated by brief bursts of guitar feedback, the track builds slowly, repeating the pattern with the tempo gradually increasing until the band are in full atonal ska-punk thrash mode. Graham's rather disorienting and stomach-churning guitar racket heard towards the climax was achieved by manually detuning the bottom string while going mad on his Cry Baby wah pedal. Add to that John Smith's mixing desk EQ manipulation, and the effect is akin to a dive-bomber going down in a ball of flames.

To non-Blur aficionados, 'Intermission' can be identified as featuring in Edgar Wright's 2017 film *Baby Driver* – used in an impeccably timed scene showing an attempted heist on a post office. It was possibly the image of a car losing its breaks (and the resulting crash) – which the music conjures cerebrally – that prompted director Wright to consider placing the track in his motor-themed flick. For Blur fans, it's remembered best as the opening theme to the documentary *Starshaped*, where it's played over a black and white montage of cheerfully chaotic tour footage, giving the piece an almost *Carry On*-esque comedic bent.

The final version, as heard on ***Modern Life Is Rubbish***, is actually a demo cut with John Smith at Matrix in January 1992, Stephen Street later deeming it worthy of inclusion. Despite the obvious gleeful abandon on display here, Food boss Dave Balfe despised the track – all the more reason for the guys to lobby for its inclusion on the album.

'Sunday Sunday' (Albarn, Coxon, James, Rowntree)

A-side single. Released 4 October 1993. UK: 26

This jolly cockney knees-up of a ditty came from a mirror opposite of the place that it portrays. While on the infamously miserable US tour of 1992, Damon spent one dreary Sunday afternoon stuck in a Minneapolis hotel room, watching from his window the spirit-sapping goings-on at the local shopping mall across the way. Prompted to write the song there and then, the lyric he came up with was an acerbically-witty take on the typical British ritual of roast dinners and afternoon snoozes played out every week on the Christian day of the Sabbath.

The song's first recording occurred upon the group's return to England – with XTC's Andy Partridge at Church Studios, Crouch End. This version (called 'Sunday Sleep') eventually saw the light of day on the *21* box set, and was a slower, gentler, meandering affair that bowled over neither band nor label. Because of this failure – and Dave Balfe's lack of trust in Stephen Street – the definitive version was recorded with the producer of 'Popscene' and 'She's So High', Steve Lovell.

Opening with huge stomping salvation-army drums (that Graham wanted to keep in for the track's duration), the intro is comparable to a proud army veteran marching down the street in full regalia. The track then settles into a pop-rock strut not dissimilar to Small Faces' 'Lazy Sunday' or The Kinks' 'Autumn Almanac'. Expanding on Damon's old-school Anglocentric lyric imagery of mother's pride, bingo halls, soldiers and *Songs of Praise*, the arrangement is augmented with a parping, parochial brass section, courtesy of The Kick Horns.

A big commercial concern of Food's Dave Balfe was the unhinged double-time middle section. He exclaimed, 'When was the last time you heard a hit single that sped up in the middle?!' But the section galvanises the piece, adding a dynamic that Andy Partridge's version sorely lacked. Here, Graham is let loose on slide guitar, while Damon gets his head down over the bingo organ, creating a delightfully deranged passage that shows their reverence for off-kilter prog-punk outsiders Cardiacs.

In spite of Balfe's reservations, 'Sunday Sunday' was eventually released as the album's third single and became the LP's highest UK chart entry, hitting number 26. This was an encouraging sign, considering the track had been available on its parent album for five months.

'Oily Water' (Albarn, Coxon, James, Rowntree)

Basking in the success of *Leisure*'s number 7 album-chart placing, Blur headed back into Matrix in October 1991 to demo some new songs. Feeling relaxed and temporarily free from Dave Balfe's scrutiny, the results of these sessions (which also produced 'Resigned' and 'Bonebag') built on the band's more esoteric and experimentally-charged side, which had previously reared its head on B-sides like 'Luminous' and 'Inertia'.

Self-produced with engineer John Smith, Damon conjures imaginative lyrical images that were sorely absent from the previous album – not to mention bringing more robustly realised states of panic and anguish:

> In a sense of self in decline
> Growing fat on sound
> It's only an early morning dream
> And the whole world will be alright
>
> My heads hurts with suspicion
> I'm coming home sometime
> I've swallowed too much oily water
> It's slipping down my spine

Like with 'Repetition' on *Leisure*, the song is sung through a megaphone, adding to the tense, gritty atmosphere. Graham's effects-pedal work is also in bloom; the disorienting, strobe-like rhythmic intro immediately grabbing the listener's attention. The unusual sound was achieved by having two guitar tracks each using a Boss tremolo effect, both set to different speeds, panned hard left and right, switching on/off/on simultaneously in the chord sequence. Graham's also responsible for the hypnotic siren-like final section at 2:57, which required him to tune all the guitar strings to E, put the wah-wah pedal at a half-open position, and overload the reverb, thus eliminating any dry signal.

The band were thrilled with the results, Alex proclaiming the track to be 'gratuitously nasty and My Bloody Valentine all over'. Though only intended as a demo, all concerned judged the recording as perfect; thus, it was included on *Modern Life Is Rubbish* as-is (albeit remixed by Street), making it the oldest track to be included on the record. Anyone who was later surprised at the volte-face the guys pulled off between *The Great Escape* and *Blur*, obviously hadn't paid much attention to 'Oily Water'.

'Miss America' (Albarn, Coxon, James, Rowntree)

Another track that wouldn't have been out of place on 1997's *Blur*. Cut at Matrix in December 1991, this is a peculiar-sounding recording, with ultra-dry vocals up-front in the mix, and a rumbling lo-fi, over-compressed ambience – perhaps the result of the chaotic circumstances it was recorded in.

After laying down a basic rhythm track of acoustic guitar, bass and vocal, the group decamped to the nearby Plough pub to celebrate their friend and publisher Mike Smith's transfer from MCA to EMI Publishing. While the rest of the band subsequently ventured out to watch a Pulp concert, Graham went back into Matrix and recorded various overdubs on the piece. When Smith and the rest of the group returned to the studio later that evening, they found the guitarist in a state of extreme inebriation, performing a percussion part by hitting a chair leg with a small piece of wood. Smith's entry into the studio caused Graham to drunkenly shout 'Michael!', captured along with the resulting laughter at the track's beginning.

The track possesses a vague jazz flavour thanks to Alex's walking bass runs and Graham's woozy-bluesy clean-tone electric guitar parts. It was actually Damon who came up with the novel alternate guitar tuning, which features the high E-string tuned down to D, and the B-string down to A.

The lyric is a gentle, poetic affair, with Damon crooning about an all-American woman who 'sits in the shower, plucking hours from the sky', before romantically intoning 'I love only you'. Written in 1991 in the aftermath of Blur's first US tour, 'Miss America' was a cautiously optimistic first glimpse of Damon's love/hate relationship with that country – a relationship which, in 1992, was about to septically sour.

'Villa Rosie' (Albarn, Coxon, James, Rowntree)

Recorded during the same October 1992 sessions when Steve Lovell produced 'Sunday Sunday', 'Villa Rosie' is further proof that, by now, Blur were gradually developing their definitive British guitar-pop sound – replete with Damon's tough 'cockney geezer' lead vocal and some decidedly XTC-ish 'woo hoo' backing vocals.

The subject matter concerns an imaginary gentleman's drinking club where 'all losers' were welcome, with the promise of a 'sweeter life'. The imagery also reflected Damon's time living around Clapham in 1987:

> Across the common every day, you come across the fine line
> But wearing boots can prevent the leeches in the long grass

Elsewhere, the quirky cartoon credo on display is almost like a precursor to the screwball philosophising that would later be utilised to such winning effect on the 'Parklife' single:

> Practice doesn't make perfect when you're interbreeding
> Speaking drivel, can it get confused with heavy breathing?

Musically, Graham is in fine form as ever – his fiddly, fidgety fretboard hammer-ons working brilliantly during the main guitar hook at 0:21. Also of technical note is his brief solo at 2:38, where engineer Jason Cox is credited with the 'small stone operation', which basically involved turning the phaser effect pedal rate knob as Graham played. Then there's the madness of the twin intro and middle section (2:01-2:17), where Alex uses a bottleneck slide on his bass, for extra chaos. Graham recently stated that these sections remind him of Brian May's guitar cacophony at the beginning of Queen's 'Death on Two Legs'.

Though not a key song in Blur's catalogue, 'Villa Rosie' was nevertheless a successful attempt at moving forward with their new English classic-pop aesthetic, and must've come as a welcome relief after the aborted Andy Partridge sessions.

'Coping' (Albarn, Coxon, James, Rowntree)

In November 1992, this was the first *Modern Life Is Rubbish* song to be recorded with reunited producer Stephen Street. Like 'Sunday Sunday', it was originally attempted with Andy Partridge a few months before. That version – arguably the most successful of the tracks taped with the XTC man – was a looser, rockier affair that also benefitted from a faster tempo. Unfortunately, that arrangement – despite its undeniable vibrancy – was rather unfocused, and eventually, the band decided they should re-record the song.

The Stephen Street version does lack the energetic excitement of Partridge's effort, but it is more tightly constructed and streamlined. Featuring a looped, Krautrock inspired motorik drum rhythm, and a retro Jupiter-8 synth hook played by Damon, this rendition puts more emphasis on the song's overt pop sensibilities. The spiky intro guitar riff and monotone verse melody are in the same ballpark as 'Advert' and 'Colin Zeal' respectively, whilst Damon's lyric paints the picture of a man trying to stave off an impending nervous breakdown:

> I'm too tired to care about it
> Can't you see this in my face?
> The emphasis is on coping

Upon hearing Street's completed production, Food's Andy Ross claimed he could hear a 'career-saving single'. Optimistic perhaps, but the staccato-fuzz-guitar-meets-euro-synth texture did lay the groundwork for future big Blur pop moments, particularly 'Girls & Boys' and 'Stereotypes'.

'Turn It Up' (Albarn, Coxon, James, Rowntree)

The most old-school Blur *Leisure*-like track on *Modern Life Is Rubbish* was originally demoed in 1991 at Matrix, during the same sessions as 'Oliy Water' and 'Resigned'. It was re-recorded with Stephen Street in late 1992, and included on the album at the insistence of Food. 'Turn It Up' was seen by Dave Balfe as the only track on the record that had the slightest chance of doing well in America.

But it was never a serious contender for a US single, and sits awkwardly as the album's penultimate track, hamstrung by its nonsensical and banal throwaway lyrics:

Kazoo Kazoo you are mine
Kazoo Kazoo every time

Soon after the album's release, members of Blur were quick to dismiss this ultra-upbeat track. Graham explained to *Select* in 1995: 'When we wrote it, it seemed like a good jangly pop song. But it turned out to be an middle of the road rock song. It didn't have any peculiarities, so we were turned off by it.'

Damon was blunter about the situation, calling the song 'crap', and wishing it wasn't on the LP. Of course, he's right about it being a mistake to include the song, but it certainly possesses a sparky charm with bags of energy and an undeniably hooky chorus. Also, Dave pulls off a few drum kit heroics towards the end, in much the same vein as his work on 'Wear Me Down'. Perhaps 'Turn It Up' might've been better suited to being a TV commercial for a stereo system or background music for a montage of exciting goals on a *Match of the Day*-type football show! Or, as it turned out, not.

'Resigned' (Albarn, Coxon, James, Rowntree)

This wonderfully-lugubrious affair was taped in November 1991 at Matrix with John Smith, during the same sessions that produced 'Oily Water' and 'Bone Bag'.

Graham's shimmering 'Gimme Shelter'-style guitar arpeggio opens the track before the rest of the band come in with a melodica-dominated groove that foreshadows the following year's 'Blue Jeans'. Possibly due to the band being in a 'psychedelic state of mind' during its creation, the track gets more and more spaced out as it floats along, with Graham leading proceedings. During the elongated melodica solo, he lets loose with a variety of trippy sonic flavours, firstly combining two Rat effect pedals with a flanger to create a Robert Fripp-influenced Van der Graaf Generator guitar fuzz field. As the track fades out, there's some Syd Barrett-inspired slide guitar noise fed through a tremolo pedal.

Damon's sorrowful lyrics are pensive, with a vocal melody to match, romantically forlorn and delicate, and the little harmony over the line 'Only you can fill my blank heart' demonstrates this sadness perfectly.

I think too much
On things I want too much
It makes me hateful
And I say stupid things

Once again, deemed worthy of inclusion on *Modern Life Is Rubbish* despite only being a demo, 'Resigned' was first heard outside the band's circle when it was released in a limited edition of 2000 cassettes given away at the Food Records Christmas party at Brixton Academy on 21 December 1991. It then appeared the following February on an EP created to promote the upcoming

Rollercoaster Tour (with Jesus & Mary Chain, My Bloody Valentine and Dinosaur Jr.), providing the song with a lot of early exposure, and proving the band were quite proud of their recent foray into melancholia.

'Commercial Break' (Albarn, Coxon, James, Rowntree)

Formally known as 'The Outro', this was recorded at Matrix in January 1992 in the same session as companion piece 'Intermission', and was tacked on to the end of the album after 'Resigned'.

Made up of three brief sections, this instrumental is the album's shortest track, clocking in at just 58 seconds. Opening with a Karl Orff-inspired six-note tip-toeing prance suitable to accompany a cheeky cartoon burglar, the piece then climbs through ascending diminished chords, setting up the second section: a punky thrash using the same melody and chord sequence. Then we're treated to a quick gallop of maniacally-changing major chords, before it abruptly ends.

Evidently – and perhaps fuelled by their usual ritual of having a few beers in the Plough pub before commencing recording – the boys are having supreme fun here, revelling in a mischievous streak that came to fruition on the next album *Parklife*.

Contemporary Tracks

'Popscene' (Albarn, Coxon, James, Rowntree)

A-side single. Released 30 March 1992. UK: 32

'Hey, hey, come out tonight!' sang Damon for the first time, on stage at the Kilburn National on 24 October 1991. Those in attendance were treated to the debut performance of Blur's next single after 'Bang', and their only official 1992 release.

Recorded with Steve Lovell at Matrix in February 1992 (Stephen Street was out of favour with Food after 'Bang''s disappointing chart performance), 'Popscene' was an exciting new direction for the group, heralding a new confidence and a punky swagger, light years away from the passive baggy stylings of their previous few singles.

Opening with Graham's viciously-lacerating fuzz-flanged one-note guitar riff, the rhythm section then rudely butt in with Alex's grinding bass and Dave's hard-hitting rhythm based on Can's 'Mother Sky' (Graham's suggestion). The track really explodes into life at 0:37 with a gnarly horn arrangement from The Kick Horns: the first time brass had ever been used on a Blur recording. Add to all this Damon's aggressively-scornful vocal – which launches a bilious attack on the industry he'd come to deride – and the band had entered completely new territory.

> A fervoured image of another world
> Is nothing in particular now

And imitation comes naturally
But I never really stopped to think how
And everyone is a clever clone
A chrome-coloured clone am I
So in the absence of a way of life
Just repeat this again and again and again

Expectations were high. Both band and label expected 'Popscene' to be a huge hit, so when it limped to a UK chart peak of 32, all involved were dumbfounded and the boys were deeply wounded. Following the eventual release of *Modern Life Is Rubbish*, they refused to include 'Popscene' on the album, with Graham saying, 'If you didn't fucking want it in the first place, you're not going to get it now'. But Blur fans *did* want it – only the industry the song lambasts, didn't.

Many now attribute the single's failure to the then-recent emergence of the Seattle-derived rock genre known as grunge. The movement was, of course, spearheaded by the all-conquering Nirvana, who'd just released their 30-million-selling second album *Nevermind*. In 1992, Blur were seen as unfashionable baggy has-beens who were sorely out of step with current trends, and 'Popscene' – despite its title – was nowhere near poppy enough to burst grunge's commercial bubble. But Blur would get there.

'Mace' (Albarn, Coxon, James, Rowntree)

B-side of 'Popscene'

Recorded just before 'Popscene' in early-1992, 'Mace' relates to an incident in the bands Seymour days, when they were on a support bill at Dingwalls, Camden. The band got into a drunken altercation where bouncers maced them – agonisingly – in the eyes. Momentarily blinded, the band were escorted to casualty, where, in the waiting room, an elderly woman berated them for necking vodka.

Conversely, the composition itself is unremarkable, with a linear structure devoid of dynamic variety. The rather tame vocal melody is faintly bolstered through some mysteriously-odd lyrics, though they are not obviously relevant to the source of inception:

Pedalling on a bicycle I'm on my way to make a call
I fall asleep and dream of burning down the house

More successful are Graham's guitar overdubs – an early example of his delay-pedal trickery – which plant seeds for flowering on future cuts: particularly 'On Your Own'. Alex – whose bassline demonstrates the same distorted menace as The Stranglers' Jean Jacques Burnell – described 'Mace' as a 'bash-it-out-after-tea job'.

'Badgeman Brown' (Albarn, Coxon, James, Rowntree)

B-side of 'Popscene'

This curiously decrepit-sounding piece was originally written for the soundtrack to an unmade film which was intended to be directed by legendary Hipgnosis album cover designer Storm Thorgeson. Alex remembers that the story was about 'a man walking out of his house and just vanishing'. But in the end, the movie was unrealised.

Recorded in December 1991, the song was directly inspired by Thorgeson's childhood friend Syd Barrett; the eerie half-shouted, half spoken-through-a-megaphone verses ('calling from a lonely hill') landing like an icier version of his Pink Floyd composition 'Vegetable Man'. Meanwhile, the gentler passages melodically resemble 'Late Night' from Barrett's 1970 LP *The Madcap Laughs*. Not surprisingly, Food Records detested the track, with Andy Ross telling *Select*: 'If ever Blur got too cocky or we began to think too highly of them, we'd play 'Badgeman Brown' to remind us, and them, that they were in fact human.'

'I'm Fine' (Albarn, Coxon, James, Rowntree)

B-side of 'Popscene'

Amateurish at best, here we have a Seymour-era recording that was taped during the same 1990 Roundhouse demo sessions that produced 'Sing'. The two songs could not be further removed from each other, in both quality and style. 'I'm Fine' has a strong 1960s pop flavour, with Graham's 12-string guitar employing a Byrdsian jangle, while Alex produces a rubber-souled sub-McCartney bass line. Similarly, Damon's 'I'm just fine' chorus line – with Graham's added harmonies – is perhaps a reference to The Beatles' 'I Feel Fine'. Unfortunately, the lyrics are blandly inane and the vocal melody uninspired: 'I do what I do/I do it again/Again, again, again'.

A far superior beefed-up rendition – titled 'Always' – was recorded in 1991 with Stephen Street. Featuring a tighter, tougher rhythm section and some ornate reverse guitar from Graham, this second version subsequently surfaced on the *21* box set. It begs the question: why didn't they use that version on the 'Popscene' B-side instead?

'Garden Central' (Albarn, Coxon, James, Rowntree)

B-side of 'Popscene'

When Beastie Boys were guest-reviewing singles for the *NME* in April 1992, they rather damningly declared that this creepy wordless track should've been the A-side over 'Popscene'. Disingenuous or not, that was not what the Blur boys would've wanted to hear.

Recorded in January 1992, 'Garden Central' (originally called 'Garden Centre') is a trance-like instrumental developed from Graham's vaguely wild-west-sounding guitar riff. Tripped-out further with reverberated slide guitar, Damon and Graham's distantly moaning aahs and oohs complete the eerie ambience. Perhaps one of the least-known recordings in the entire Blur catalogue, it could've been the perfect surreal addition to a David Lynch movie soundtrack.

'Into Another' (Albarn, Coxon, James, Rowntree)

B-side of 'For Tomorrow'

A distinctly *Chairs Missing*-era Wire-influenced B-side (their 'French Film Blurred' comes to mind), 'Into Another' was written and demoed in early 1992 under the working title 'Headist'. Recorded at Matrix with John Smith, the oblique verse lyrics ('It makes a whistle with a twistle/But no one can hear') give way to a chorus evoking the image of someone surrendering to yet another hangover. Indeed, Graham was known to be drinking a bottle of vodka a night on the Rollercoaster tour.

Instrumentally, an intriguing element is Damon's use of the Clavinet (an electrically-amplified Clavichord) put through a quick delay on high repeat, giving the verses a sharply-throbbing electrical pulse. There's also a quasi-pastoral guitar section at 2:21-2:32, sounding as though Graham had been listening to a lot of 1960s psychedelic folk from the likes of Pentangle and The Incredible String Band.

'Peach' (Albarn, Coxon, James, Rowntree)

B-side of 'For Tomorrow'

'Peach' is an ethereal acoustic tune, laid down during the same January-1992 sessions that produced 'Mace'. Quite unusually for a pop/rock song, it features prominent use of the harmonium – an antiquated foot-pump-operated reed organ used most famously on The Beatles' 'We Can Work It Out' and 'Being For The Benefit Of Mr Kite'. Damon bought the instrument in Clapham, with Alex humorously commenting, 'It cost about five pounds, and then he spent about a thousand doing it up'. However, Graham's succulently sustained and full-bodied electric guitar tones moved the piece into a realm beyond that of your typical acoustic ballad, contributing to the broken-record effect at the song's close.

The lyrics match the music's ghostly vibe, appearing to deal with the subjects of madness and murder:

A gun in your pocket
And hair in a locket
From the girl you once loved
Where is she now?
You've gone crazy

The repeated lines 'You've got a gaping hole in your head / I'd let the birds nest there instead' presumably allude to the possibility that the protagonist had then turned the gun on himself.

Despite – or maybe because of – the dark subject matter, 'Peach' became a favourite on US college radio. Years later, Damon maintained that it was still an enjoyable song for him to 'strum along to'.

'Bone Bag' (Albarn, Coxon, James, Rowntree)

B-side of 'For Tomorrow'

Buried treasure in the Blur discography, this was recorded in November 1991 during the same fruitful sessions that produced 'Resigned', and shares that song's romantically-mournful mood – Graham confessing he enjoys Damon's soppier side.

The introduction's exotic percussion is an Indian tabla sample, programmed by Dave, who then retreated to the nearby Plough for refreshment. Returning a few hours later, the song was finished, proving that when they were on a creative roll, Blur could really achieve a lot.

Due to engineer John Smith's accommodating exploratory presence on the session, there's also an obvious psychedelic ambience, with heavily-flanged vocals and two out-of-phase tremolo guitars contributing to the sleepily-stoned atmosphere.

Unused for eighteen months until its inclusion as a 'For Tomorrow' B-side, 'Bone Bag' was eventually performed live at Peel Acres (home of the legendary DJ John Peel) in a September 1999 Radio 1 session. Gliding effortlessly into the set between '1992' and 'Trimm Trabb', it showed just how much this era in Blur's history informed the introspective experimental brooding found on *13*.

'Hanging Over' (Albarn, Coxon, James, Rowntree)

B-side of 'For Tomorrow'

With shrieks of feedback followed by a sludgy, circling three-chord riff over a 1960s backbeat, this is the closest Blur ever came to resembling *Bleach*-era Nirvana. Also, Damon's verse vocal sounds not unlike Pete Shelley of Buzzcocks.

Written in 1991 – around the time Damon started his relationship with Justine Frischmann – the song title and lyrics such as 'I feel a pain in my head' and 'I shouldn't have ever got out of bed' hide no clues as to what the song is about.

A decent if unspectacular effort, there are a couple of idiosyncrasies that up the oddity factor, such as the unexpected key change from B to C# occurring at 2:24, not to mention a strange unidentified adenoidal noise towards the end conjuring an image of Donald Duck on helium. Even more strangely, Food's Andy Ross wanted to include the track on *Modern Life Is Rubbish* – perhaps he was pre-hanging over.

'When the Cows Come Home' (Albarn, Coxon, James, Rowntree)

B-side of 'For Tomorrow'

Notwithstanding the melancholic majesty of 'Resigned', this jaunty romp would've made the perfect closer to the album, and compared to nearly all its other B-sides, the clarity of arrangement and lyrical wit stand out like a sore thumb.

Written and recorded alongside 'For Tomorrow' in early-1993, it's a crisp Stephen Street production. With a four-note opening brass motif, the musical roots lay in the bouncy music hall pop that The Beatles put to use on tracks like 'When I'm Sixty-Four' and 'Maxwell's Silver Hammer'.

Featuring Damon's Tommy-Steele-esque *cheeky-chappie* lead vocal and some cutesy Beatle-aping chorus backing harmonies, there's little room for Graham, Alex and Dave to spread their wings instrumentally. Instead, they admirably play backup band to Damon, proving the guys were just as adept at serving a song as they were at flexing their musical muscles. In fact, Alex's bass doesn't even come in until the final verse.

Unfortunately, the track didn't make the album's final cut. With lyrical references to Food boss David Balfe's attitudes to finance, it's thought that he twigged that the song was about him, and thus naturally refused to entertain its inclusion on the record.

Don't listen to the accusations that you're tight
You could be the first man on your street to get it right

It's a shame, as the writing is sharp and it feels like a natural fit alongside tracks like 'For Tomorrow' and 'Sunday Sunday'. Indeed, Graham later lamented, 'It was horrible trying to cram the tracks on ... it could have been an eighteen-track album', and the song was also a favourite of Damon's mother: Hazel Albarn. Nevertheless, it remains a noteworthy piece in Blur's history due to its lyrical content, making it an undoubted predecessor to the Balfe-inspired 'Country House'.

'Beachcoma' (Albarn, Coxon, James, Rowntree)

B-side of 'For Tomorrow'

A languidly-subdued Syd Barrett-esque jewel, 'Beachcoma' appears to be a sister piece to 'Luminous' – similar aurally and with a complementary poetic flavour:

I'm in mine and mine is fine
I'm wrapped up in shining days
Barefoot in summertime

Despite being recorded in late-1991, the song actually dates back to the previous year. Written around the same time as 'There's No Other Way', 'Beachcoma' was then known simply as 'Hole'.

Notable sonic touches on this John Smith-engineered recording include Dave's gated snare drum hits and a plethora of overlaid guitars ranging from 'Oily Water'-esque howling, to the deep, fast and gentle tremolo-swathed plucking in the verses. In the end, there was such an abundance of guitar parts on the recording, that Graham had to draw a visual song map to make sense of all the concurrent parts.

Though ultimately too esoterically-delicate to ever be in serious contention for the album, the song would've undoubtedly been a centrepiece of the band's proposed spring-1992 version of a second album – nestled in amongst tracks such as 'Bone Bag, 'Into Another' and 'Peach'.

'Es Schmecht' (Albarn, Coxon, James, Rowntree)

B-side of 'Chemical World'

The last original B-side to be recorded for the *Modern Life Is Rubbish* campaign, Damon wrote this on a May-1993 trip to Germany with Alex in order to promote the album. The title itself is a misspelling of the German expression 'es schemkt': meaning 'It tastes good'.

Recording was undertaken later that month at Ritz Rehearsal Studios in Putney, on an eight-track portastudio that Damon had purchased from Andy Partridge. Damon acknowledged the track as the band's most lo-tech recording yet, and it was commendably engineered by none other than Dave Rowntree.

Experimental and krautrock-like in nature, the track is certainly Can-influenced, with a rhythmic pulse akin to their track 'Shikako Maru Ten', and lyrical references like 'Waltzing on an autobahn' bringing glimpses of Kraftwerk. Graham's stabbing-staccato guitar riff, weaves in and out effectively with Alex's busy Holgar Czukay-inspired bass runs, while the daft, babbling saxophone squeaks are actually Damon on a keyboard.

'Young and Lovely' (Albarn, Coxon, James, Rowntree)

B-side of 'Chemical World'

If there was ever a poll for Blur's greatest-ever B-Side, surely this would be a contender for the crown. A strikingly mature piece of writing for a twenty-five-year-old, it's an astute and gloriously-melodic rumination on the moment a proud parent watches their pride-and-joy leave to make their mark on the world. Wise beyond its years in the same way as The Kinks' 'Where Have All The Good Times Gone', it wasn't until the band performed the song at the 2012 Olympics closing ceremony at Hyde Park that Damon and the band – as parents of teenagers – acknowledged how the song finally made sense to them.

Produced by Stephen Street at Maison Rouge in the same sessions as 'Chemical World', the track contains Damon's confidently-sung vocal in the grand balladeering style of Scott Walker, while Graham's folky hammer-on guitar lines draw a parallel to his work on 'Tender'. He later confessed that this was some of the most heartfelt guitar he had produced to date, and who could argue.

The fact that the track was left off *Modern Life Is Rubbish* is nothing short of a minor tragedy. With the heartfelt 'We all know why, why you do it' refrain towards the end pulling from the same emotional well as future standouts like 'The Universal' and the aforementioned 'Tender', the song really is as good as anything on Blur's second album and could've even been a single. Food records were apparently keen on placing the track on the album, but due to its late arrival and Dave Balfe insisting on including 'Turn It Up', the band just couldn't agree on what else to cut from the record – thus 'Young And Lovely' was left out in the cold. If Blur do ever release an official B-sides album, this will be an undisputed highlight.

'Maggie May' (Stewart, Quittenton)

B-side of 'Chemical World'

This Rod Stewart smash was the first cover that Blur ever recorded. Having returned broken and exhausted after their summer-1992 US tour, the band were offered the chance to contribute to a three-CD charity compilation called *Ruby Trax – The NME's Roaring Forty*, given away to NME readers. Artists involved were asked to cover a number-1 single from the last 40 years. Why Blur chose 'Maggie May' remains unclear.

Recorded with Steve Lovell at Matrix in June 1992, the session marks the only time Alex James refused to play on a Blur record: claiming to hate Rod Stewart. The bass was played on a keyboard, the remaining trio bashing the song out with little fuss – and notwithstanding Graham's distinctive wah-wah solo, little finesse too. Unbelievably, Food Records considered putting this plodding rendition out as a single, showing just how out of touch they were with the group's idea of who *they* were and where they were headed creatively.

'My Ark' (Albarn, Coxon, James, Rowntree)

B-side of 'Chemical World'

A late-1960s blues-rock pastiche in the same vein as – but less dynamic than – *Leisure*'s 'Wear Me Down', 'My Ark' was recorded in October 1991 around the same time the group demoed 'Popscene'. Clocking in at almost six minutes, the track bops along harmlessly with a soft, hazy vocal delivery from Damon, who mumbles, 'I've got time to build you up so tall, you won't fall down on me'. Graham's rising Hendrixian riffing is the track's most effectual aspect, though even *he* described it as a bit of a dull number. Damon has claimed it reminds him of 1960s San Francisco acid-rockers Blue Cheer, but Dave's estimation of 'Lenny Kravitz drinking a cup of tea' is more accurate.

'Mixed Up', 'Dizzy', 'Shimmer', 'Fried', 'Long Legged', 'Tell Me, Tell Me' (Albarn, Coxon, James, Rowntree)

B-sides to 'Sunday Sunday'

Recorded in 1989 and engineered by Beat Factory owner Graeme Holdaway, these Seymour demos are a fascinating glimpse of the band in their embryonic stage. Highlights include the punky stomp of 'Fried' (performed live at the 1999 B-sides gig) and the vaguely-psychedelic drone piece 'Shimmer'.

'Daisy Bell (A Bicycle Made For Two)' (Dacre)
'Let's All Go Down the Strand' (Castling, Murphy)

B-sides of 'Sunday Sunday'

Running out of B-sides, the band decided to tackle these two vaudeville standards, offering a glimpse of where heads were at in the summer of 1993. As evident in the recent composition 'When The Cow's Come Home', Damon was increasingly in thrall to British music hall, with the rest of the band more than happy to champion British terminology and history in their new recorded output.

Both songs were recorded one Sunday afternoon at Maison Rouge in a party-like atmosphere replete with friends and acquaintances that included Justine Frischmann: Damon's girlfriend and Elastica's singer. 'Daisy Bell' stays faithful to its original arrangement until the chorus, when it launches into a brutish punk swagger with the whole rowdy mob joining in on gang vocals. Graham delivered the faux English-gentleman spoken-word section at 1:43 through a megaphone.

'Let's All Go Down The Strand' proceeds in a similar merry fashion, except without the tempo changes or punky thrashing, Graham even providing some delicate mandolin-like guitar textures in the final verse. A third song – 'For Old Times Sake' – was apparently recorded, but Damon came in early one morning to erase it from the tape, suggesting that perhaps by then, the band and their coterie had indulged in too much revelry.

'Wassailing Song' (Trad.)

One-sided 7-inch single. Released 16 December 1992.

Damon and Graham originally sang this medieval Christmas carol when they were in the Stanway Comprehensive School choir. (Not to be confused with the similarly-titled and more popular 'Here We Come A-Wassailing' – a wassail being a wooden bowl that holds hot punch). Humourously credited to Gold, Frankincense And Blur on its 7" pressing, only 500 copies were ever produced. Given away for free at a December-1992 gig at The Hibernian in Fulham (an Irish nightclub, 200 yards from Maison Rouge studios), the vinyl is now a collector's item.

Unique in the Blur catalogue for being the only recording where each band member takes a lead vocal (in this order: Damon, Graham, Dave, Alex), the track thumps along on Dave's bodhrán like tom-toms, with only a simple lone accordion for company. Numerous backing vocals bolster the arrangement, with Damon showing off his impressive bass vocal range, hitting an effortless low D when harmonising in the chorus and humming in the verse.

For those not lucky enough to possess the 7", the recording is best-known as musical accompaniment to footage of Blur visiting Stonehenge during Glastonbury 1992: captured in the tour documentary *Starshaped.*

'Seven Days' (Albarn, Coxon, James, Rowntree)

Released 30 July 2012 in the 21 box set.

Another of the tracks recorded at Church Studios with Andy Partridge in 1992, this boasts a cheerful panpipe keyboard riff, quirky guitar textures and tight Syd Barrett-esque vocal harmonies. Unfortunately – and rather like the other two songs attempted with the XTC man – the arrangement is rather incoherent and the tempo could do with being increased a touch. It's a decent enough piece though, and one wonders why Stephen Street wasn't later given a crack at producing it.

A live version recorded in April 1992 for Radio 1's *Evening Session*, was released in 2000 as the B-side of 'Music Is My Radar'. Featuring a more dreamy, shoegaze-type ambience, this rendition is more reflective of the original demo.

'Never Clever' (Albarn, Coxon, James, Rowntree)

Released on the Food 100 compilation in 1997, and on the 21 box set.

A rarity in Blur's discography, this was originally intended as the follow-up single to 'Popscene', before Food wisely scrapped the idea. Despite possessing a muscular rocking energy, the tune isn't particularly memorable, nor are the lyrics distinguished. This early-1992 Matrix demo pales in comparison to the live rendition released as one of the 'Chemical World' B-sides. Aggressively deranged, it was recorded during Blur's chaotic appearance at that year's Glastonbury Festival.

Parklife (1994)

Personnel:
Damon Albarn: Lead and backing vocals, Keyboards, Moog, Melodica, Vibraphone, Recorder, Programming
Graham Coxon: Guitars, Backing vocals, Clarinet, Saxophone, Percussion
Alex James: Bass, Lead vocal on 'Far Out'
Dave Rowntree: Drums, Percussion, Programming
Stephen Street: Synthesizer, Sound Effects, Programming
Phil Daniels: Narration on 'Parklife'
Laetitia Sadier: Vocals on 'To the End'
Stephen Hague: Accordion
The Kick Horns: Brass
The Duke String Quartet: Strings
The Audrey Riley String Quartet: Strings on 'To the End'
Recorded August 1993-January 1994 at Matrix, Maison Rouge and RAK Studios
Producers: Stephen Street, Stephen Hague, John Smith, Blur
Release dates: UK: 25 April 1994, US: 14 June 1994
Label: Food/Parlophone (UK), SBK (US)
Chart placings: UK: 1, US: did not chart

Though selling modestly and receiving little in the way of press attention or airplay, *Modern Life Is Rubbish* had provided Blur with a much-needed sense of purpose and identity. Subsequently, it became evident during their August 1993 Reading Festival appearance, that a massive grassroots fan base had developed, with punters spilling out of the packed second-stage tent during the passionately-electric performance. Tellingly, Damon later recalled the post-gig press interview in which he had the editors of *NME* and *Melody Maker* sat either side of him, both smitten. It seemed that the tide was finally turning in Blur's favour.

Despite this upturn in fortunes, the band were still skint and in serious debt to Food Records. It was make-or-break time. Sensing their last shot at glory, the guys spent summer 1993 feverishly demoing new material in batches of two and three, with sessions proper beginning at Maison Rouge in August. Keenly focused, and with confidence in their rapidly-evolving abilities skyrocketing, the band (aided by Stephen Street) were flying, with the record finished by early-1994.

The last hurdle was Dave Balfe. Following the previous year's unpleasant run-ins, relations with the Food boss became fractured, with the guys preferring to liaise with his more avuncular partner Andy Ross. Balfe's final contribution to the Blur story was in trying to get them to name the upcoming third album *London*, and place a fruit and veg cart on the cover. Thankfully, the band resisted, and Balfe sold his stake in Food Records shortly before the album's release.

Eventually named *Parklife* (working titles included *Magic Arrows*, *Soft Porn* and *Sport*) and featuring its now-iconic Stylorouge-designed greyhound racing cover, the album crashed into the UK album charts at number-1 upon its April 1994 release. Having missed the boat with *Modern Life Is Rubbish*, the stunned UK press clamoured to declare the record a supremely intelligent, multifaceted work, and the benchmark against which all new British pop should be measured. For once, they were right. Propelled by the massive singles 'Girls & Boys' and 'Parklife', it stayed in the upper reaches of the UK album chart for the next eighteen months, eventually selling a staggering 1.2 million copies there alone. Finally – after three albums and four years of toil and trouble – Blur had entered their imperial phase and were on top of the world.

Today, *Parklife* is widely-regarded not only as Blur's finest work but as one of the era's defining albums – a cultural touchstone for British music in the 1990s, paving the way for countless other young guitar bands to enter the mainstream pop arena in its wake.

'Girls & Boys'

A-side single. Released 7 March 1994. UK: 5, US: 59, US Alt-rock: 4

Starting out as a fun distraction after temporarily giving up on the recording of the song 'Parklife', Stephen Street had a feeling 'Girls & Boys' would be a huge moment for Blur. And it was.

In the summer of 1993 – after a particularly tough twelve months – Damon took a well-earned holiday to Magaluf, Majorca, with girlfriend Justine Frischmann. While there, he found himself fascinated when observing the hordes of young vacationing Brits, frequenting, as he put it, the 'tacky Essex nightclubs'. In a simultaneous state of awe and disgust, he found the experience revelatory. He told the *NME's* Paul Moody in 1994: 'I love herds. All these blokes and all these girls meeting at the watering hole and then just copulating. There's no morality involved. I'm not saying it should or shouldn't happen'.

Returning home, Damon wrote the song, the band demoed it, and then took it to Stephen Street. He immediately heard a hit. Up to this point, Street usually sought authorisation from Food Records before undertaking any Blur recording, but not this time. Excited, and sensing a surefire smash, they began work on the track before the label even heard the demo, with Street mixing it immediately. Initially angered by this rogue move, Food's Andy Ross soon softened his attitude after hearing the results.

Built around one chord sequence of Gm/C/F/Eb/Gb/F repeated *ad infinitum*, the track starts with an instantly recognisable burbling-octave synth intro, before the rhythm section lunge in at 0:16. The programmed drums are at the classic 1970s Chic disco tempo of 120 bpm, providing a robotic vibe with just a few live cymbal overdubs: it was book reading day for Dave. Add to this Alex's brilliantly swaggering Duran Duran-esque bass line, and – much like with 'There's No Other Way' – you can tell we're in hit single territory from the rhythm section alone.

So far, so pop. What makes this recording so stylistically original is the introduction of Graham's guitars to the party – inspired by the likes of post-punk bands Wire and Gang Of Four. Jabbing into the mix at 0:48, they create an angular, scabrous flavour – like someone angrily scrawling graffiti over a piece of Bauhaus art – ripping through the glossy mechanical sheen. Other intriguing sonic elements include a series of high-pitched tremolo-infused three-note licks at 2:24, and the slow-flanged white noise often occurring in the verses and choruses, giving the immense effect of a Magaluf-bound jet plane flying by.

On top of it all are Damon's deceptively-smart lyrics. The tongue-twisting yet insanely catchy chorus contains allusions to the inversion of sexual roles, in much the same way as The Kinks' song 'Lola':

> Girls who want boys
> Who like boys to be girls
> Who do boys like they're girls
> Who do girls like they're boys

Versus 'Lola':

> Girls will be boys and boys will be girls
> It's a mixed-up muddled-up shook-up world

The verses directly depict the bawdy scenes witnessed in Magaluf, taking an ambiguous, non-judgemental stance on the predicament of the typical full-time reveller, 'avoiding all work 'cause there's none available'. Meanwhile, Damon's vocal delivery is camp and adenoidal, possessing the common touch – a perfect aural accompaniment to the lyric's gender-bending hedonistic imagery.

It all wrapped up into a perfect single package. The biggest irony of all was that Blur had finally made the kind of track that Dave Balfe had wished they would make for years, and now he was selling his stake in Food and leaving the company. Indeed, his ex-business-partner Andy Ross later admitted it was a 'blatantly-contrived hit: a sales pitch for the whole album'. In that sense, it seems that Damon had the last laugh.

Upon release, 'Girls & Boys' crashed straight into the UK singles top 5, paving the way for parent album *Parklife* to hit number 1 a few weeks later. Blur's lives had changed forever, and their imperial phase as one of Britain's biggest guitar groups of the 1990s was about to begin.

'Girls & Boys' is still one of their best-known and biggest-selling singles, having sold 400,000 copies in the UK alone; also racking up an impressive 100,000,000 Spotify streams. When Radiohead played a BBC Maida Vale session in 2003, an audience member asked vocalist Thom Yorke if there were any songs he wished he had written. 'Girls & Boys' was his reply.

'Tracy Jacks' (Albarn, Coxon, James, Rowntree)

Following the previous album's character study 'Colin Zeal', 'Tracy Jacks' is a Ray Davies-esque *name* song – like 'David Watts' or 'Johnny Thunder' – chronicling a middle-aged civil servant who slowly loses the plot, bulldozes his house and then runs into the sea, in his birthday suit.

This stylistically-diverse cut opens with a bubbling synth invoking a gently-rippling pool, before Graham's Pete Townshend-esque Bsus4 power chord cannonballs into the calm water. The rhythm section settles into a 'Honky Tonk Women'-type rhythmic swagger, complete with cowbell and a strutting Alex bass line. Then the verses give way to a military drum rhythm in the 'Every day he got closer' sections, with a tight upper harmony from Graham, who also sings the 'Tracy Jacks' vocal refrain. Keeping with the water/sea theme, he also gives an excellent guitar interpretation of a squawking seagull (at 2:28), achieved with a long-quaver delay set to the song's tempo of 123 bpm, mixed with a phaser effect pedal. The Duke String Quartet bring a sophistication and grandiosity to proceedings – at 4:09, pulling off The Beatles' 'Glass Onion' trick by performing a mournful slow fade-out.

Lyrically, it's likely that Damon got the idea for the protagonist's name from Terry Jacks – singer of one of Damon's all-time favourite songs: 'Seasons In The Sun'. Also, the lines 'stood on the seafront ... threw his clothes in the water' were inspired by the opening titles of the popular British 1970s sitcom *The Fall and Rise of Reginald Perrin*, in which the lead character fakes his own death by leaving his clothes on the beach. Incidentally, the beach mentioned in verse two is that of Walton-on-the-Naze – an Essex seaside town about 20 miles from where Damon and Graham grew up in Colchester. Damon told *Select* in 1995: 'They fascinate me, all those dead seaside towns on the East coast. Walton... Frinton. They have one guesthouse and it's boarded up. It's a couple of council estates, a few old houses and the bleak, bleak North Sea. They're half-places.'

Interestingly, the CD booklet has a drawing by Graham of a balding man in a floral dress, ready to strike a golf ball. Though this gives the impression that Tracy Jacks is a transvestite, nothing of this is mentioned in the lyric.

'End of a Century' (Albarn, Coxon, James, Rowntree)

A-side single. Released 7 November 1994. UK: 19

The fourth and final *Parklife* single is a delightful reflection on the prosaic nature of how we as a society spent our evenings leading up to the new millennium: merely six years away at the time. Damon elaborated further, saying, 'It's about how couples get into staying in and staring at each other. Only, instead of candlelight, it's the TV light.'

One of the last tracks recorded for the album, Stephen Street has cited this song as a fine example of Damon 'getting the art of songwriting really sorted'. Possessing a chirpy McCartney-esque melody, the first verse opens with a reference to an ant infestation that Damon and his girlfriend Justine once encountered in their Kensington flat:

She says there's ants in the carpet
Dirty little monsters
Eating all the morsels
Picking up the rubbish

Other standout lines include, 'The mind gets dirty as you get closer to thirty' and 'We kiss with dry lips when we say goodnight', and Graham's multi-layered contrapuntal chorus harmonies add sweetness to the melancholic whimsy.

The track coasts along on a solid mid-paced groove, underpinned with acoustic guitars and a chugging electric rhythm part on the downbeat. Alex's simple, stately bassline fills gaps in the vocal with pretty three-note runs, while Damon plays a vintage organ set to the flute preset. It's most effectual during the vaguely psychedelic intro and middle breakdown, which switches its time signature to 3/8. The icing on the cake comes from the Kick Horns' Richard Edwards' wistful trombone solo at 1:26, returning again during the final section.

'End of a Century' was cast as Blur's 1994 Christmas single, incidentally up against Oasis' similarly-paced effort 'Whatever'. After the huge success of 'Girls & Boys' and 'Parklife', the 'End of a Century' chart placing of 19 was a disappointment for Andy Ross, who later remarked that 'This Is a Low' should've been chosen instead. He has a point perhaps, but even then, I doubt that moody and magnificent epic would've fared much better given the nature of the 1994 singles chart. Regardless, 'End of a Century' was one of the album's many standout cuts, and is still a much-loved bittersweet symphony in Blur's rich discography.

'Parklife' (Albarn, Coxon, James, Rowntree)

A-side single. Released 22 August 1994. UK: 10

One of the most iconic releases in Blur's career was almost left on the cutting room floor. Demoed in May 1993 at Ritz rehearsal studios in Putney – during the same self-recorded sessions that produced 'Es Schmecht' – 'Parklife' had regularly been performed live that summer and aired on a Radio 1 live session with DJ Mark Goodier in July. Damon wrote it living on Kensington Church Street, inspired by mornings walking through nearby Hyde Park. When the band reconvened with Stephen Street in August to start the album, all present agreed that this rather quirky song about dustmen, pigeons and joggers, smelt like a hit – except they couldn't get it right.

Feeling the pressure of making a single, Street strove to make the track as tight as possible, and originally used a loop of Dave playing a 4-bar drum rhythm to a click, with a pronounced emphasis on the toms. With this rather rigid rhythm track and Damon's ultra-exaggerated faux-cockney verses, the group were struggling to nail the arrangement, and Street began to tire of the track. They decided to shelve it and move on.

As the album sessions progressed through the autumn, the band recorded a waltz-like instrumental called 'The Debt Collector', which Damon was intending to write a spoken-word poem for. Wanting an authentic cockney accent for it, and wary of the rather unconvincing portrayal he'd already attempted on 'Parklife', Graham suggested reaching out to actor Phil Daniels. Though a childhood hero of Damon and Graham's after starring as Jimmy in the movie *Quadophenia*, Daniels had never heard of the group, but agreed to come down to the studio. The problem was, Damon couldn't think of a single word for 'The Debt Collector'. Scrambling at the last minute to accommodate the actor who was on his way to the studio, Damon decided to have him try narrating 'Parklife' – an event that caused the song to immediately spring back to life.

As a born-and-bred working-class London lad – and a decade older than Damon – Daniels had the perfect voice for the track, giving the verses an authentically good-natured *joie de vivre*. Surprising the band by turning up with long scraggly hair and a beard (he was appearing as Jigger the vagabond in the musical *Carousel* at London's Shaftesbury Theatre), it took just three takes to nail the part. Graham recalled that Daniels even decided to pronounce the 'h' in the line 'there will always be a bit of my heart devoted to it', making it sound even more adorable. All involved were delighted.

Galvanised by Daniels' star turn, the group excitedly went about completing the track. Dave added a looser, more lively drum part over the original rhythm, supplying just the right amount of jaunt and swagger, and then completed his contribution by smashing plates, to simulate the sound of breaking glass. The single was back on.

Arrangement-wise, the track is choc-full of memorable moments. First, there's Graham's now-famous opening guitar riff, not to mention the wondrously dexterous flowing chorus pattern and the augmented B chord arpeggio at the end of each chorus.

Secondly, Alex's bass line featuring the tritone interval is also distinctive. To cap it all off, Graham's chants of 'Parklife!' (sounding like The Jam's 'Eton Rifles'), and Damon's anthemic sing-along chorus vocal with harmony backups, are irresistible.

Then there are the peculiarities: bizarre 'n' bonkers elements you'd never expect in a top-10 single. At 2:15 – after the line 'It's got nothing to do with your Vorsprung durch technique, you know', Graham plays a snatch of the German national anthem on saxophone. Proficient on the instrument after taking lessons at school, it's the first time he ever played one on a Blur recording. Other strange occurrences include the garbled vocal inflexions sprayed liberally at various points, and the lyrics themselves – 'a morning soup', 'brewers droop', 'gut lord marching' – all barking-mad.

But somehow, it all created magic. Released as the album's third single, it shot to number 10 in the UK, going platinum, eventually shifting over 600,000 copies (good for Daniels, as he opted to take a royalty over a fee). Featured in countless TV shows and commercials, 'Parklife' became part of the fabric of British culture in the mid-to-late 1990s and one of the defining songs of the entire Britpop movement. Ray Davies – one of Damon's songwriting heroes – has voiced his admiration for the track, and The Massed Bands of the Household Division performed the song at the closing ceremony of the 2012 Olympic Games.

'Bank Holiday' (Albarn, Coxon, James, Rowntree)

A ferociously high-octane ode to those regular national vacation days, 'Bank Holiday' was another song that debuted live in June 1993 on a Mark Goodier BBC radio session, albeit in a more sluggish fashion than the eventual album version.

Though one of the more lightweight compositions on *Parklife,* it's conversely also the heaviest, featuring a frantic rhythm akin to thrash-metal punks doing the conga. In fact, the tempo was so rapid that Damon had to record two overlapping vocals in order to squeeze the words in. With lyrics referencing grandma's dentures, barbecues, lager, fun pubs and the uniformly empty appearance of all national high streets, the song is a sardonic and humorously accurate portrayal of what a working-class 1990s-British bank holiday was actually like, complete with a clarion call for the dreaded back-to-work blues: 'A-G-A-I-N.'

Instrumentally, the guitar playing is as agile as ever, with Graham performing nimble-fingered chord arpeggios in the intro, whilst impressing producer Street with his effect-pedal work in the verses, which involved hitting a fast vibrato on and off for less than a second at the end of each phrase. Dave gives one of the most brilliantly breakneck drum performances of his career, with his slowly-rising drum fill at the song's climax (1:30), an obvious arrangement highlight.

'Badhead' (Albarn, Coxon, James, Rowntree)

Following the palette-cleansing rush of 'Bank Holiday' comes the album's first emotionally charged song. A delicately low-key affair, it's like a continuation of 'Blue Jeans', appearing to deal with the aftermath of a love affair. Here we find Damon in a wearily-detached mood, forlornly singing:

> And I might as well just grin and bear it
> 'Cause it's not worth the trouble of an argument

His fatigued state of being is accompanied by a restrained yet ornate band arrangement, which opens with a melancholy brass intro. The rhythm section keep it simple, with Dave playing a soft, steady brushes rhythm, and Graham chiming a tick-tock twelve-string guitar lick. Damon – whose pirouetting verse organ parts add a certain baroque flavour – is credited with playing a real Mellotron during the 'And I know' breakdowns.

For all the instrumentation's evident sorrow, the pretty chorus' 'oooh' backing vocals sweeten the atmosphere somewhat. And best of all, Graham's elegantly-understated guitar break at 1:50 brings to mind George Harrison's exquisite tone on *Abbey Road* tracks like 'Something' and 'The End'.

Keeping in line with the song title, Graham was to describe 'Badhead' as 'Good for a hangover like Nick Drake is good for a hangover. There's nothing abrasive about it.' In that sense, it's probably why this smoothly sumptuous track is an undervalued minor gem in the ranks of Blur's ballads.

'The Debt Collector' (Albarn, Coxon, James, Rowntree)

Opening with Damon shouting 'Ready then!', followed by Graham's 'One Mississippi, two Mississippi…' count-in, this instrumental waltz showcases Damon's effortless gift for melody. With a delightfully-whimsical brass and woodwind arrangement from the Kick Horns, the piece was originally intended to have words. The group approached actor Phil Daniels to narrate it, but Damon couldn't think of any words, so Daniels ended up on the song 'Parklife' instead.

It was recorded live at Maison Rouge with Damon on organ, Dave on brushes and Alex on bass – Alex attesting that only a single bass note was dropped in later. Graham played the acoustic guitar simultaneously with the tambourine by stomping on it like a busker would, apparently to mimic the ambience of a Tom Waits track.

Unsurprisingly, Blur rarely performed 'The Debt Collector' live, but it was the opening song at their 1995 Mile End gig – Damon coming out on stage dressed as an old man, wearing an oversized suit, with a potbelly, wig and face mask.

'Far Out' (Albarn, Coxon, James, Rowntree)

An unlikely eventuality in Blur's history is the fact that Alex managed to beat Graham to having a song of his own and singing a lead vocal on a Blur album, especially as he never sang backing vocals on stage.

'Far Out' was originally recorded at Maison Rouge in autumn 1993 as a faintly glam, up-tempo rock stomper. Food's Andy Ross – who was fond of this version and wanted it on the record – claimed it was Damon who vetoed the track's inclusion on *Parklife*. In the book *3982 Days*, he said: 'I don't think Damon was too happy about Alex getting credit for a song that didn't have that much to do with him, and he applied a lot of pressure to not have it on the album ... Alex didn't want to stand up for himself.' But Damon couldn't have been *that* against the song, as the band re-recorded it at Matrix in January 1994, two weeks after 'This Is a Low' was completed. Consequently, 'Far Out' was the last song recorded for *Parklife*.

It opens with a spooky wobbling atonal acoustic guitar passage from Graham, who then seems to mumble, 'Don't just whisper it, Alex, c'mon'. Then Damon enters with a similarly strange organ phrase while Dave trills on the congas, setting up tension before the song settles into its slow spaced-out groove.

The lyric is very much in trippy early-Pink Floyd Syd Barrett territory (specifically 'Astronomy Domine'), as Alex proceeds to sing two bewitching verses listing numerous moons, stars and planets:

Vega Capella, Hadar
Rigel Barnard's Star
Antares, Aldebaran, Altair
Wolf 359, Betelgeuse

As the band were unsure how to end the song, producer Stephen Street put filtered tape-echo on Alex's final word, creating the slowly disintegrating 'sun-sun-sun-sun' fade-out.

Alex eventually finished and remixed the original up-tempo version with producer Ben Hillier in 1999, and it surfaced as a soundtrack to footage of the Beagle 2 space project on Blur's 'No Distance Left To Run' single DVD.

'To the End' (Albarn, Coxon, James, Rowntree)

A-side single. Released 30 May 1994. UK: 16

The second *Parklife* single was a new addition to the band's stylistic armoury. Having already nailed so many genres – including alt-dance, punk, synth-pop, orchestral pop and psych – Blur had now mastered the big ballad. When Damon sat at the piano to play the song for the others, its sophistication and emotional power blew everyone away.

Roping in Damon's girlfriend Justine Frischmann to sing the choric French vocal, the band cut a demo with John Smith in October 1993 at Matrix. Strangely, when Food Records heard the recording, they decided to bypass the now firmly-established producer Stephen Street. Looking for the right person to conjure an elegantly epic soundscape for the track, production duties were handed to Stephen Hague, who'd previously worked with Pet Shops Boys and New Order. Naturally, this would've irked Street somewhat.

Ironically, Hague felt that most of the demo was good enough to keep as it was (including the majority of Damon's lead vocal), so his production responsibilities boiled down to just adding overdubs. But what overdubs they were. Audrey Riley (Muse, Foo Fighters, Smashing Pumpkins) arranged the soaring, romantic John Barry-esque strings, while Hague played some chromatic accordion runs. Laetitia Sadier from the band Stereolab replaced Frischmann's vocal with a smoky, sultry Gallic authenticity. The band had considered other French chanteuses such as Charlotte Gainsbourg and Francoise Hardy – who, incidentally, later sang on an alternate version subtitled 'La Comedie', recorded at Abbey Road and released on the 1995 'Country House' single.

The backing track features Dave's soft looped drum rhythm, with the snare drum in the disengaged position. Alex and Graham keep things simple with gentle, rhythmic bass and clean guitar parts respectively, and Damon's vibraphone overdub supplies a perfectly pregnant introduction.

Damon's impassioned lead vocal was reportedly performed while stoned during the Matrix demo session, a remarkable occurrence considering it was one of the very best he'd yet committed to tape. The lyrics are also exceptional, portraying visions totally at odds with your standard love song. Detailing a couple unsuccessfully trying to navigate a troubled spell in their relationship, one wonders whether this and the similarly melancholy 'Badhead' were reflections on struggles Damon and Justine may have already been experiencing.

All those dirty words
They make us look so dumb
Been drinking far too much
And neither of us mean what we say

Released as *Parklife*'s second single, 'To the End' charted at 16 in the UK; a slight disappointment after the top 5 success of 'Girls & Boys'. Perhaps too candid a love song to be serious hit material, 'To the End' nevertheless drew strong emotion from the band members. Alex openly wept when he heard the finished mix, while, more publicly, it was at the end of this song that Damon broke down in tears during Blur's triumphant 2009 Glastonbury Festival reunion concert. It seems that this achingly sad yet beautiful piece was a personal affair after all. What isn't in any doubt, is that it's one of *Parklife's* supreme achievements and one of the groups best ballads: up there with 'The Universal' and 'Tender'.

'London Loves' (Albarn, Coxon, James, Rowntree)

In much the same way as 'Tracy Jacks', 'London Loves' is a triumph of arrangement – a series of effervescent moments that make the recording shine. It opens with a bleeping, blipping synthesizer sound inspired by the taught synth line in 'Genius of Love' by Talking Heads-offshoot Tom Tom Club. In an extremely hungover state, Dave sequenced the sound on a portable Yamaha QY10 acquired in San Francisco on the 1993 US tour.

The Talking Heads comparisons don't end there, though, because the track, in general, has a certain 'Psycho Killer' groove to it, particularly in the chorus, where Graham's stabbing guitar rhythm is kindred to Tina Weymouth's throbbing 'Psycho Killer' bass intro. Speaking of Graham and effervescent moments, he's full of them on this recording. Most obvious is the elastic, distorted solo at 1:43 – inspired by his love of Robert Fripp's guitar work. In the book *3862 Days*, Graham said, 'For 'London Loves' I used the same effects box that Fripp would've used on 'Fashion' by David Bowie. My solo was modelled on that solo. I always liked that style, and Streety liked it. Big fat notes going on forever.'

Graham's other masterstroke was the taut eight-note staccato verse phrase. Difficult to play, it required the guitarist to mute the strings while striking them in a rapid up-and-down motion.

Damon's immersion in the 1989 Martin Amis novel *London Fields* (in particular, uncouth antihero Keith Talent) shines through lyrically, especially in the lines 'The lights are magic, and he feels lucky, and he's got money, shoots like an arrow'. Those in sport often call darts arrows, and Keith Talent was a keen 'dartist', prompting the album's working title *Magic Arrows.*

The chorus line 'The misery of speeding heart', held particular significance for Damon, as shortly after the 'Girls & Boys' single was released, he began to suffer panic attacks; a malady that lasted into the following year.

Other bits of sparkle come in the form of the 'oh-wah-oh' Buggles backing vocals at 1:59, and the 'oooohhh, hey! hey!' pre-chorus buildup at 2:41, which Kaiser Chiefs later expanded to ridiculous proportions on their Stephen Street-produced hits 'I Predict a Riot' and 'Oh My God' from 2004. Finally – and presumably as a nod to the line 'Coughing tar in his Japanese motor' – on the morning of mixing, Damon taped the traffic report heard in the fade-out from the now-defunct Greater London Radio.

'Trouble in the Message Centre' (Albarn, Coxon, James, Rowntree)

In September 1993, initial *Parklife* sessions were halted when the band went back out on the road for autumn shows in Britain, Japan and America. When sessions restarted in December 1993, the first song recorded was 'Trouble in the Message Centre'. Damon's writing process was evident in the *Parklife* CD booklet, which included his original New York Wellington Hotel room receipt (dated 7 December), complete with scrawled lyrics and chords. Some of the phrases – 'message centre', 'local and direct', and 'room to room' – were taken from the hotel room telephone buttons, and the line 'So just strike him softly away from the body' was a slogan on a book of matches.

The track is a chugging, new-wave-ish piece, which Graham confirms was influenced by Magazine's 1978 single 'Shot by Both Sides' – and thematically, possibly Blondie's 'Hanging on the Telephone' from the same year. Neither Stephen Street nor Food's Andy Ross were particularly enamoured with the new song – the former feeling it 'lacked melody'. While Street is correct, that's not the point – too much melody would puncture the icily dark and detached mood.

Still, there's plenty to quench the thirst of those with a penchant for hooks and harmony. It opens with a staccato piano figure slowly fading in – kind of like a ghostly cousin of the 'Advert' intro – before the band crashes in with punk menace. Another engaging part is Damon's addictive distorted synth verse lines, providing a welcome tune against the monotone vocal.

Chordwise, there are some affecting key changes, occurring between the G major verses and Bb minor choruses, and Graham's guitar solo moves up further to Bm, creating a triumphant middle eight complete with Damon's now customary 'la la la la la''s.

Perhaps due to the muted reception from producer and record company alike, Blur rarely played the song live until 2015, when it featured prominently on their world tour for *The Magic Whip*.

'Clover Over Dover' (Albarn, Coxon, James, Rowntree)

Never played live until a surprise March 2019 one-off Africa Express gig at The Circus in Leytonstone (in which Dave was relegated to congas), this song sees Blur enter baroque pop mode.

Opening with a seagulls sample taken from Stephen Street's vintage BBC sound effects album, it's a 1960s-influenced harpsichord-driven piece, with Dave's drums even panned to one side like on a Kinks or Beatles recording from the period. Admittedly, the arrangement is stronger than the song, but this doesn't spoil it. Graham's reoccurring ascending guitar arpeggios and the main riff at 0:20 are a smooth-'n'-silky delight, while Damon's harpsichord adds a grandiose sophistication.

Unusually for Damon post-*Leisure*, the lyrics conjure images of emptiness and suicide, and possibly were inspired by the final scene in the *Quadrophenia* movie – in which Jimmy (played by Phil Daniels) rides his scooter to the Dover cliffs – before the bike flies off the edge without its distressed rider:

I'm on the white cliffs of Dover
Thinking it over and over
But if I jump, it's all over
A cautionary tale for you

However, despite the blankly-dour subject matter, the song is a light and winsome moment of respite on an otherwise heavily cerebral album, and thankfully its original incarnation as a ska track was jettisoned in favour of this pleasing adaptation.

'Magic America' (Albarn, Coxon, James, Rowntree)

A scathing attack on American culture, Damon justified the song in a 1994 *Melody Maker* interview: 'I feel physically unwell when I'm in America. I can't help that I have this Americaphobia. I had to write that one seething little song and get it out of my system.'

Seething it may be, but it's also a wickedly funny pop song with enough quirks and hooks to outweigh any bad feeling. It begins with a mini-collage of random noises (the first of which engineer Jason Cox sampled from TV) set to a sampled hi-hat rhythm, before Graham's spiky guitar arpeggios lead into the first verse, introducing us to the character Bill Barratt. Named after the huge British property-development firm Barratt Homes, he's a small-town dweller who dreams of an alluring life of glitz and glamour on the other side of the pond.

The lyric offers up sarcastic visions of a place with 'shopping malls' and 'buildings in the sky', where '59 cents gets you a good square meal', all courtesy of 'the people who care how you feel'. Damon has since revealed that most of these lines were phrases used in adverts. Elsewhere, there's a cheeky, giggling keyboard solo from Damon, which Graham compares to the soundtrack of the 1970s British cartoon *Roobarb and Custard.*

In recent years, fascinating footage of the band recording 'Magic America' (and other *Parklife* tracks) – filmed on Stephen Street's camcorder – emerged online. Featured in the clip is Graham recording the verse guitar part on his butterscotch-blonde Telecaster; a cheerful Damon listening to Alex's bass take (with guide vocal audible), and more humorously, the guys standing around the mic singing their 'la la la la la' group chorus, with Damon berating Alex for getting it wrong, shrieking, 'It's easy!'.

'Jubilee' (Albarn, Coxon, James, Rowntree)

When Food's Andy Ross considered 'This Is a Low' as a single over 'End of a Century', he was perhaps overlooking the potential of the thumping 'Jubilee'. The closest Blur had yet come to glam rock with a punk attitude; it's a Sex Pistols-meets-Mott The Hoople belter, complete with a rousing chanted chorus:

He dresses incorrectly, no one told him seventeen!
He not mean enough
He dresses incorrectly, no one told him seventeen!
He not keen on being like anyone else

Born in the Queen's Silver Jubilee year of 1977, and therefore seventeen when the song was released in 1994, the protagonist is a long-haired jobless teenage lout who's 'gone divvy' from 'too much telly', and is forever 'scabbing' from his father 'Billy Banker'. These scornful lyrics are all delivered in Damon's best Ian Hunter/Bowie drawl, with vowels strangulated to an almost comic degree, while the verse melody bears a resemblance to the 1978 Cheap Trick hit 'Surrender'.

Elsewhere, more Mott the Hoople comparisons can be drawn from the 'Golden Age of Rock 'N' Roll' saxophones that come in after the 'He not mean enough' lines, and the verse staccato piano riffing which came from 'All the Way From Memphis'. The rhythm section drives hard and tight throughout, with Graham's supple Les Paul guitar verse lines and his Steve Jones-ish punk-boogie chorus guitars amping up the excitement. Another arrangement touch of note occurs during the 'He plays on his computer game'; the electronic bleeps were not some vintage Space Invaders-type video game, but a hand-held toy designed to relieve stress for traffic-stricken motorists.

Recorded at Matrix in July 1993 (with the saxes added later), the immensely fun 'Jubilee' was one of the earliest tracks recorded for *Parklife* album, and despite its non-single status, the band performed it triumphantly on *Top of the Pops* in February 1995, shortly after they picked up an unprecedented four Brit Awards in one night.

'This Is a Low' (Albarn, Coxon, James, Rowntree)

Arguably *Parklife*'s artistic peak – and certainly a watershed moment in Blur's creative history – this magisterial backing track was recorded bang in the middle of the album sessions. The song started life with only four words – 'We are the low' – but the band thought enough of Damon's basic melody and chord structure to attempt a full arrangement.

Beginning with the unsettling sound of a slowed-down tape wobbling away, while a mysterious reverse drum loop fades in, the song starts proper with Graham's moody guitar arpeggios, which pause briefly before leading into the main action. With a brooding unhurried tempo, the piece ebbs and flows in waves consisting of Dave's live drums played over the reverse loop and Alex's relaxed bass slotting between in the lower register. Graham's passionate guitar solo that slowly burns through in the middle eight (played on a vintage Gibson ES-335), is actually a simultaneous blend of three different takes, including one where he is sitting in front of his Marshall stack with the volume turned up to the max. Another brilliantly atmospheric touch is the recurring divers-breathing sound effect, presumably added at the mixing stage as a device confirming the lyric's nautical theme.

Knowing they'd created an instrumental epic of glorious proportions, the recording then sat in the vault while they finished the album. With sessions breaking up for Christmas 1993, Damon still had no lyrics other than those initial four words. Rather like the Christmas before when he wrote 'For Tomorrow' under huge pressure, everyone was desperate for him to come up with the goods on his festive break. He spent that holiday with his parents in a Cornwall cottage and walked out on the cliffs every night with the backing track playing on his walkman, trying to spark something in the imagination. Eventually, ideas came from his immediate surroundings, connecting the word 'low' with visions of coastlines and meteorology, but still, he had no words.

Fast-forward to 4 February 1994, the *Parklife* sessions were wrapping up and Damon still had nothing to sing – stubbornly refusing to include the track on the album. Stephen Street was getting concerned that this mighty work wasn't going to make the cut. Sensing a musical tragedy, he harried Damon into getting the lyric done that night so they could record it the following day, the penultimate of the sessions. Finally acquiescing to Street's demands, Damon sat up through the night and wrote the words, with a little help from a handkerchief he'd received as a Christmas present from Alex. On it was a map of Britain and all of the sea regions used on the BBC shipping forecast. Starting at the Bay of Biscay, Damon worked his way around, choosing various places he made evident in the lyric ('Dogger Bank', 'Lands End' ', Tyne, Forth and Cromarty'). Incidentally, the shipping forecast can be heard at the beginning and end of the *Starshaped* tour film, and the band used to listen to it when on tour in America to remind them of home.

The chorus now made dual sense – the low-front described in weather conditions, and the more obvious connotation of a low mental mood. The next day – despite having a hernia operation booked for later in the afternoon – Damon went into the studio early with Street and John Smith to record his lyric.

Footage of this extraordinary vocal session is captured on Stephen Street's camcorder film. Showing Damon perched high up on a stool with three lyric sheets hanging in front, he looks out the control room window onto the Fulham streets, strumming gently on Graham's precious 335 as he sings.

Later on, after just coming 'round from the anaesthetic, a heavily-sedated Damon made a phone call to Maison Rouge to instruct the band and Street on how he thought the song should be mixed. Though he was described as extremely lucid, Damon now has no recollection of this. Then, in the final mixing stage, Graham added those ghostly high chorus backing vocals.

Finally, the track was complete, and bar a re-recording of 'Far Out', so was the album. Alex and Graham have both stated that the song has a certain opioid influence, and though it's too early in the timeline to assume that Damon had delved into this area of drug use, the song does have a similar nocturnal ambience to 'Beetlebum', which was unequivocally heroin-inspired. So, musically at least, this is a stepping stone to Damon's late-1990s life.

Seen as a Blur classic today, the song has been performed at all major concerts since its release and even appeared on the *Blur: The Best Of* compilation in 2000 – the only non-single to do so, proving its special place in the hearts and minds of its creators.

'Lot 105'

An instrumental piece that began shows on the *Parklife* tour (as evident on the Alexandra Palace *Showtime* video), 'Lot 105' was so named from the auction where Damon purchased the song's lead instrument: a £150 vintage Hammond Organ. Beginning with a delightfully cheesy built-in samba drum pattern, the keyboard melody enters soon after and is the star of the show, giving the track its main focus and sounding like incidental music on some garish 1970s game show. Soon the rest of the band join in – Dave with a cowbell, tambourine and maraca combo, Alex and Graham shimmying along cheekily together, dancing a fruity bass-and-guitar fandango. Then there's a sudden change of pace at 0:53 – Dave counting in the band for a punk thrash in the style of 'Intermission', with some 'Wa la la la la' gang vocals.

Though nothing more than a great ball of flippant fun, 'Lot 105' was placed at the very end of the album, coming twelve seconds after 'This Is a Low'; that track seen as too heavy-duty a way to close the LP. It was Graham who came up with the only lyric: '18 times a week love!', likening the track musically to 'Barbara Windsor coming along to take you up the arse'.

Contemporary Tracks

'Magpie' (Albarn, Coxon, James, Rowntree)

B-side of 'Girls & Boys'

A peppy pop-rocker crammed full of vibrant detail, 'Magpie' was recorded sans vocal around the same time as 'Starshaped', in December 1992 during the *Modern Life Is Rubbish* sessions. The reason for Damon not completing a lyric then could partly have been down to Dave Balfe's despondent reaction, deeming the track's stop-start rhythms as 'Too confusing for Americans'.

Graham thought this track sounded in places like a throwback to the *Leisure*-era days of baggy. Indeed, Dave's verse drum pattern has a certain skippy, semi-dance-rock feel, and Alex's funky bass sits on top, in a similar fashion to tracks like 'High Cool' and 'Bang'. Conversely, Graham's parts come across as an attempt to destroy that notion – bristling with angular innovation, from the main refrain's descending distorted hook line to the chaotic twisting melange of atonal noise peppering the fade-out.

When the track was dusted off for the *Parklife* sessions, Damon still had trouble coming up with a lyric, in the end completely lifting the verses from William Blake's 1794 poem 'The Poison Tree' (uncredited on the 'Girls & Boys' single). The vocal in these verses treads a similar megaphone-wielding path to 'Badgeman Brown', but this time, thankfully, there's more melody, and the choruses benefit from a galvanising three-part harmony stack on 'I'.

'Anniversary Waltz' (Albarn, Coxon, James, Rowntree)

B-side of 'Girls & Boys'

This was originally recorded as a jingle for the Simon Mayo Show on BBC Radio 1 and was later performed on the same July 1993 Mark Goodier session as was 'Parklife', under the pretentious working title 'Why Is the Time Signature of 3/4 Obsolete in the Late 20th Century?'. Intended for inclusion on *Parklife*, it was wisely decided that 'The Debt Collector' waltz was enough.

Still, 'Anniversary Waltz' is oddly amusing, with Graham's unusual bending lead guitar lines being of particular interest. Filmed on Street's camcorder, it shows the inventive way Graham achieved the sound – plucking the 2nd string 7th fret with his right index finger from the 16th fret, bending the note up, then hammering down on the 16th fret and releasing the bend, creating a strange comedic effect akin to a squeaky door swinging back and forth. Elsewhere on the video, we see Graham play a saxophone melody, and Damon playing what appears to be a duck whistle, which is, sadly, buried low in the final mix.

'People in Europe' (Albarn, Coxon, James, Rowntree)

B-side of 'Girls & Boys'

A kind of baby-brother piece to 'Girls & Boys' (right down to the octave synth part), this is a lighthearted scoop of high-camp Eurodisco, complete with a tacky, gormless programmed drum track. Though recorded with Street in the middle of the *Parklife* sessions, it was never in the running for inclusion on the album.

The verses are made up of a series of random multi-language words and phrases, which were the result of the band racking their brains for as many foreign expressions as possible:

> Ciao ciao bella, Monaco
> Bon voyage in Sverige
> Kom nu med, vi far dricka manana

Though this rendered the track as nonsensical froth, the 'ba ba ba ba' chorus is catchy, and the arrangement has plenty to offer, including Alex's bubbly bass, and Graham's spicy guitar lines that are sprayed throughout like hot sauce over an ice cream sundae.

'Peter Panic' (Albarn, Coxon, James, Rowntree)

B-side of 'Girls & Boys'

A favourite of producer Stephen Street, the band discussed 'Peter Panic' conceptually before a single lyric or note was written, according to Dave. Cleverly combining the carefree boy who never grows up, with a state of extreme agitation, the lyrics describe a Ziggy Stardust-alien type 'who lives forever' and came to Earth, leaving 'his secret with the chemist' before he 'disappeared to a distant star'. Presumably, what he was offering was some sort of universal remedy for depression and anxiety; a sugarcoated Prozac pill of sorts.

The track flits between soft percussion-less verses featuring Graham's swirly vibrato guitar-picking while Damon croons a gentle fairy tale lullaby. The stomping sing-along choruses are an altogether more spirited affair, and an assortment of sci-fi synth sound effects, guitar feedback and a twinkling glockenspiel bookend the track.

'Threadneedle Street' (Albarn, Coxon, James, Rowntree)

B-side of 'To the End'

This odd but enchanting recording – named after the road in Central London which hosts the Bank of England – was cut at Matrix in spring 1994 during B-side sessions for the remaining three *Parklife* singles. At the 1999 Electric

Ballroom B-sides gig, Damon described the writing process, saying, 'I didn't know what to write about, so I just looked at the business page in *The Times*'. Though meaningless when read as a whole, the lyric does conjure an alluringly-stark atmosphere riddled with financial business phraseology.

Opening with a synth-drum rhythm akin to Elastica's 'Connection' (recorded around the same time), the track's intriguing textures are bountiful. Graham's pinging high-pitched guitar arpeggios are played through an octave pedal, while the wobbly 'ooh wah lah' backing vocals are hilarious and almost menacingly off-key. Damon's double-tracked vocals are treated with a short, sharp delay, while the mix sonics as a whole are otherworldly, sounding like a prototype for the similarly unusual 'Yuko and Hiro' recorded the following year.

'Got Yer' (Albarn, Coxon, James, Rowntree)

B-side of 'To the End'

Behold another waltz! But this time, it's a menacing, circus-type one, and at 1:06, even moves away from the standard 3/4 time signature to a crafty 5/4. The unsettling track's most prevalent feature is Damon's vocal delivery – especially of the 'sour old bed pan' that is the grumpy old man. Sounding like a cross-fertilisation of John Entwistle's Who track 'Boris the Spider' and Dickens' Fagin, the protagonist is driven mad by a 'fly buzzing between his ears', before firing a shotgun at the source of his irritation; his own head perhaps? The rifle sound was achieved with a snare drum sample sped up with some falling-pitch reverb, while Graham's descending slide-guitar break has the wide grin of a Cheshire cat.

An utterly bizarre Matrix studios-recorded B-side, 'Got Yer' was afforded as a result of Blur's recent chart success. Alas, Food's Andy Ross failed to see the funny side.

'Beard' (Albarn, Coxon, James, Rowntree)

B-side of 'Parklife'

'Beard' was inspired by the snooty regulars down at The Premises in Hackney, a jazz-leaning rehearsal space that Blur used during the *Leisure* period. As Alex recalls, it was 'total cod jazz, chromatic scales with notes dropped at random. It used to really annoy them.' Dave named it under the assumption that all jazzists had beards, and Graham thought it could've also been called 'Pipe' or 'Beret'. Indeed, it's perfectly plausible that someone in *The Fast Show* comedy series writing team heard this insincere B-side and was inspired to come up with the show's Louis Balfour character.

It unfolds as a series of four freeform solos by each band member – Dave's supple stick work principally holding the arrangement together. A childhood pupil of Saturday morning jazz classes at Landermere music school in Thorpe-

Le-Soken, he also had jazz experience in his pre-Blur tenure playing with Idle Vice, a jazz-punk combo. Blur considered adding canned applause after each solo, but sadly this never came to pass.

'Supa Shoppa' (Albarn, Coxon, James, Rowntree)

B-side of 'Parklife'

A twin to 'Lot 105' – complete with vintage Hammond organ, handclaps, cowbell and Graham's offbeat staccato guitar jabs – 'Supa Shoppa' was debuted live at the Alexandra Palace show in November 1994. A jolly pleasant instrumental throwaway, it was reported that Graham's record-store-worker friend Biffo experienced goateed customers coming up to ask what this 'great tune' was playing in the shop, thus seemingly confirming the track's jazz credentials.

Further showcasing Blur's versatility, it could've easily been another contender for *The Fast Show* jazz-club sketch. Andy Ross likened it to the Italian soccer team having a casual kick-about, and the flighty, fruity flutes were synthesized. 'You don't fuck about with a real flautist on a B-side', reckoned Alex.

'Theme From an Imaginary Film' (Albarn, Coxon, James, Rowntree)

B-side of 'Parklife'

Arguably the cream of the *Parklife* B-side crop, this splendid song was – aside from Graham's sporadic nimble-fingered guitar work – largely a Damon solo effort. A lively waltz in 6/8 time, the track was recorded over a four-day spell with Stephen Street at Matrix's sister studio – Matrix 2 – in October 1993, just after the initial *Parklife* sessions halted and right before Blur flew to Japan for some shows.

The song came into being in the summer of 1993 when playwright and actor Steven Berkoff approached Blur to write a musical piece for his film *Decadence* (starring Joan Collins), an adaptation of his successful 1981 West End play. Damon was sent an early edit of the movie and proceeded to put his heart and soul into a lush, sophisticated instrumental for harpsichord, strings and choir, unlike anything Blur had created before. Though he liked the music, Berkoff insisted Damon add lyrics. A finished track with a strong vocal was delivered, but it was here that things turned sour, with Blur's publisher Mike Smith claiming Berkoff saw an early screening, and rudely pulled the song from the movie.

Presumably, it was rejected due to the lyric's old-fashioned, polite and proper imagery – totally at odds with the in-your-face theatrics and often filthy, violent subject matter of Berkoff's work:

What if I flew like a dove, dear
What if I wooed you in rhyme?

But it was his loss and Blur's gain, as 'Theme From an Imaginary Film' was as strong a composition as almost anything on *Parklife*, and was further evidence of Damon's now limitless songwriting capabilities.

'Red Necks' (Albarn, Coxon, James, Rowntree)

B-side to 'End of a Century'.

'Red Necks' is a country-and-western comedy pastiche featuring a lead vocal written and performed by Graham: the first time he'd done so on a Blur track. His surprisingly gruff Johnny Cash-style delivery brings a host of sarcastic rhyming puns from the perspective of a deep-south truck driver, while Alex continually interjects with unrelated babble containing Beatles references and paraphrases.

I get free coffee fill-ups at my favourite Denny's place
Find a couple of tea bags and I kick them in the face

Aside from some decidedly ropy DI'd guitar work, Damon provided the entire backing on a small Casio keyboard set to a built-in country accompaniment with a cheerily cheesy fiddle part. Accordingly, both Damon and Alex were under the influence of some particularly strong hashish during the making of this amusing yet rather silly recording.

'Alex's Song' (James)

B-side to 'End of a Century'

The unimaginatively strummed 'Alex's Song' was intended as a serious piece of music, but unfortunately, it ended up being the weakest *Parklife* B-Side. Alex wanted it to be a crossbreed of Manhattan Transfer and Prince, but possibly due to the band being uninterested, they unfairly sabotaged it for a laugh, making Alex's voice go (at his own estimation) all 'Pinky and Perky' (A 1950's BBC children's TV show).

His frustration is audible at 1:53, when the clearly exasperated bassist mutters, 'Oh dear'. Listen to the original demo on the *21* box set and you'll hear a superior version, with bass guitar, synth strings and a double-tracked chorus vocal. It's closer in feel to the Syd-Barrett-influenced 'Far Out', and proof that if the others had actually tried to help Alex, the song could've been much more.

STONE ROSES Glasto crisis update
17 June 1995 80p $(US)3.95
GENE ★ THE JESUS & MARY CHAIN ★ JOY DIVISION ★ THERAPY?
PAUL WELLER ★ PJ HARVEY ★ THE VERVE ★ MICHAEL JACKSON
NME
NEW MUSICAL EXPRESS
NEW BLUR EXPRESS
Britain's top band take over the NME
Blur photographed by Steve Double

OASIS: 'MORNING GLORY' EXCLUSIVE TRACK-BY-TRACK PREVIEW

MELODY MAKER

CAFE SOCIETY

August 12, 1995 75p

Blur

Exclusive interview pages 28-31

T In The Park: Supergrass ★ Elastica ★ Boos ★ Black Grape Live!

12 August 1995 80p $(US)3.95
NME
NEW MUSICAL EXPRESS
BONNY ON CLYDE:
T IN THE PARK
Festival report
BRITISH HEAVYWEIGHT
CHAMPIONSHIP
BLUR vs OASIS
AUGUST 14: THE BIG CHART SHOWDOWN
THE CRANBERRIES ★ SUGGS ★ GARBAGE ★ THE FALL ★ ISAAC HAYES

LIVE! THE STONE ROSES★TEENAGE FANCLUB★THE AMPS★DUBSTAR

MELODY★MAKER

December 9, 1995 75p

BRITPOP IN THE USA

BLUR OASIS

Will they make it in America?

Special report and Damon interview: pages 25-29

MORRISSEY WALKS OUT ON BOWIE TOUR

MARTIN ROSSITER ON THE NEW GENE SINGLE

The Great Escape (1995)

Personnel:
Damon Albarn: lead vocals, keyboards, piano, organ, synthesizer, handclaps
Graham Coxon: guitars, backing vocals, banjo, saxophone, handclaps
Alex James: bass, handclaps, backing vocals on 'Top Man'
Dave Rowntree: Drums, percussion, handclaps, backings vocals on 'Top Man'
Stephen Street: handclaps
The Kick Horns: brass
The Duke String Quartet: strings
Ken Livingstone: narration on 'Ernold Same'
Theresa Davis and Angela Murrell: backing vocals on 'The Universal'
Cathy Gillat: Additional Vocals on 'Yuko and Hiro'
Recorded: January-May 1995 at Maison Rouge and Townhouse
Producer: Stephen Street
Release dates: UK: 11 September 1995, US: 26th September 1995
Label: Food/Parlophone (UK), Virgin (US)
Chart Placings: UK: 1, US: 150

Thanks to the colossal sales of *Parklife* and an unprecedented four gongs at the 1995 Brit Awards, *The Great Escape* was the first album Blur recorded as bona fide pop stars and a household name in their home country. An unwanted side effect of this newfound celebrity was intense public scrutiny during the record's production, with fans camping outside Maison Rouge, and various press members shuffling in and out for photos and interviews. Consequently, the somewhat rushed and unfocused sessions were fraught with pressure, and though the band felt commercially and artistically confident, a strange tension hung in the air.

Initially, the guys had enjoyed their first flush of success, but cracks soon began to show. Damon spent the majority of 1994 suffering from crippling panic attacks that were largely a physical reaction to the shock of fame, and the songs he was amassing for Blur's fourth LP were becoming sarcastically detached, dark and twisted. Graham was also suffering. A Pavement and Sonic Youth-loving indie kid at heart, he rapidly began feeling disillusioned with what the band were becoming: a mainstream pop act playing to huge audiences of screaming teenagers. This and escalating alcohol use contributed to his somewhat disruptive and contrary studio presence, as Stephen Street revealed to *Uncut* in 2009: 'Sometimes I had to lay down the law if he was being particularly awkward. Once, he got so drunk in the Townhouse studio, I ended up saying, 'If you've got nothing positive to say, Graham, go home'. And he did.'

Accordingly, the resulting album is an intricately detailed tapestry of all this excess, confusion and despair, taking the razor-sharp musical vignettes of the previous two albums to their gaudy logical conclusion. Released just four weeks after the infamous 'Country House' vs 'Roll With It' chart battle with Oasis, critics ecstatically praised *The Great Escape* (working titles of which included *Sexlife* and *Darklife*) as a kaleidoscopic pop masterpiece that not only miraculously improved on 1994's model but cemented Blur's place as the decade's defining band. However, as soon as Oasis' second album *(What's the Story) Morning Glory?* began eclipsing sales of *The Great Escape*, the pendulum swung in the opposite direction – the British press swiftly dismissed Blur as soulless middle-class poseurs, whereas Oasis were hailed as working-class heroes.

Despite this unfounded and unfortunate turnabout, the album still sold spectacularly, shifting nearly a million units in the UK, and outselling *Parklife* in most of Europe. Even more encouragingly, *The Great Escape* was the first Blur album to chart in the US, setting up a significant breakthrough there for 1997's eponymously-titled fifth LP.

'Stereotypes' (Albarn, Coxon, James, Rowntree)

A-side single. Released 12 February 1996, UK: 7

Debuted live at a secret May 1995 gig at Camden's Dublin Castle, 'Stereotypes' was one of the first songs recorded for the album, and was originally considered for its lead single. The band's publisher Mike Smith saw this futuristic jagged rocker as a 'fantastic radical move forward', and the band were excited too, thinking it would be the first single. But in the end, it was usurped by 'Country House', which received an ecstatic reaction from the audience at the Mile End Stadium show.

An explosive opener for the LP nevertheless, the first sound heard is Graham's fuzzed-up guitar chord jabbing the listener awake: Blur were back. Keeping things in time underneath is Damon's sickly descending E-mu Proteus synth-module line, before the rhythm section ploughs in with a swaggering mid-tempo groove and a slinkily-sexy bass line. The guitar is thrilling and aggressive throughout, and the stop-start dynamics enhance the track's already strong rhythmic thrust.

Damon had the line 'Wife-swapping is your future' for a number of months before developing the saucy-seaside-postcard lyric featuring a jilted B&B owner – fond of wearing 'low cut t-shirts' and lingerie – being verse one's protagonist. Verse two focuses on a suburban couple living out their sexual fantasies while the folks next door passively look on. The chorus portrays a picture of quiet desperation, despite its cheery sing-along veneer:

The suburbs they are sleeping
But he's dressing up tonight
She likes a man in uniform
He likes to wear it tight

The neighbours may be staring
But they are just past caring

Yes they're stereotypes
There must be more to life

Released as the album's third single, 'Stereotypes' number 7 UK chart placing was not really a reflection on the song's popularity, but more the band's – at this point, they were almost guaranteed top ten status with every single released.

Though the track did appear on 2009's *Midlife* compilation, it was strangely absent from 2000's *Blur: The Best Of*; an overlooked cracker in Blur's box of pop fireworks.

'Country House' (Albarn, Coxon, James, Rowntree)
A-side single. Released 14 August 1995. UK: 1

One of the most famous/infamous songs of Blur's entire career was inspired by the man who so often tormented them in their early struggles with commerce-versus-art. In early 1994 – just before *Parklife* was released – Dave Balfe sold his stake in Food Records and bought a grade-two-listed four-acre nine-bedroom mansion in Bedfordshire called The Bury. Despite being critical of the *Parklife* album during its recording, Balfe was still able to pocket from its subsequent success: a fact that irked Damon, spurring him to write 'Country House'.

The song started life as a slow, mournful ballad, the remnants of which are apparent in the 'Blow, blow me out' middle eight, which was obviously a result of Damon's well-publicised depression after *Parklife*'s huge success. Although the track was to transform into something else entirely, its subtle melancholic darkness remained, with a lyric referencing the 'century's anxiety', one's mortality and the popular drug of choice for those with depression: Prozac. Dave Balfe has since stated that only verse one – with its description of a 'professional cynic' whose 'heart's not in it' – seemed to be about him, claiming that the guy who 'doesn't drink, smoke, laugh' and has a 'fog on his chest' was in fact Blur's manager Chris Morrison.

Other lyric inspiration included The Kinks, whose 'House in the Country' – from their 1966 LP *Face to Face* – explored similar themes. The Kinks were also an influence on the vocal style of 'Country House', with the chorus' cheerily-sarcastic sing-along nature – 'Oh, he lives in a house, a very big house' – reminiscent of music-hall-inflected Kinks songs like 'A Well Respected Man' ('And he's oh so good, and he's oh so fine') and 'Dedicated Follower of Fashion' ('Oh yes he is!'). Indeed, Food's Andy Ross has since asserted that any criticism of 'Country House' could also be levelled at Ray Davies.

The finished recording – which producer Stephen Street was immensely proud of – was an intricately detailed, highly sophisticated affair, and had the densest arrangement yet of any Blur single. Spitting out hook after endless hook, the track is absolutely crammed. By the time the final chorus arrives, there are three separate lead melodies alone fighting for your attention. It's a heady mix, and credit must go to Stephen Street for somehow making it listenable, let alone a hit.

Graham's guitar solo in the middle section must also be mentioned. Flitting between baroque and atonal weirdness, the double-tracked part sits queasily somewhere in the middle and is surely one of the strangest, most deranged guitar solos to ever grace a number 1 single. Directly after this, he adds a scoop of surreal oddness to the 'Blow me out' section, playing some intensely vibrated arpeggios that sound transmitted from a distorted funhouse mirror.

When the track was finally complete, Alex thought it was 'an odd one'. Indeed, there was a tussle between the band (who favoured 'Stereotypes') and Food's Andy Ross (who was keen on 'Country House') over what song would be the big comeback single. Any doubt was laid to rest as soon as 'Country House' was debuted live at the huge Mile End Stadium gig on 17 June 1995. The audience reaction was ecstatic.

What happened next is one of the most notorious events in UK pop music history. Though the success of *Parklife* had transformed Blur into Britain's biggest band, a swaggering new rock'n'roll five-piece from Manchester called Oasis were approaching fast in the rear-view mirror. Their 1994 debut album *Definitely Maybe* crashed into the UK charts at number one, and was at the time, the fasting selling debut LP ever in Britain. Add to that an increasingly successful singles run that culminated in the May 1995 track 'Some Might Say' landing at number one in the UK charts - and many in the music industry were expecting Oasis to soon overtake Blur as Britain's most popular group.

Though relations between the two had been cordial up to that point, Damon had been angered by Liam Gallagher's goading of him during the 'Some Might Say' celebratory party, with the confrontational Oasis vocalist screaming 'number fuckin one, mate!' in his face. That evening also saw Damon enjoy a dalliance with Liam's then-girlfriend Lisa Moorish - an incident that stoked the flames of hostility even higher.

When Food Records scheduled an August 21st release date for 'Country House', they were shocked to learn that Oasis' label Creation already had their new single 'Roll With It' due out the previous week on the 14th, despite upcoming album *(What's The Story) Morning Glory?* being over two months away. The Oasis camp refused to alter their plans, and Food were worried that 'Roll With It' coming out closely prior would dampen the impact of Blur's big comeback. Ever the competitor, and with the events of May still raw in his mind, Damon suggested they move the release of 'Country House' forward to the 14th and go head to head with their cocky new rivals. The battle of the bands was on!

In the weeks leading up to release day, *the NME* whipped its readers up into a frenzy, with the crassly divisive 'north v south', 'working class vs middle class' and 'straight up rock vs arty pop' aspects between the two bands catching on like wildfire across the UK media, so much so, that by the time the two singles were released, they were the main story on the national TV news. For a period of about three weeks, 'The Battle Of Britpop' (as dubbed in the press) was the biggest talking point in the entire country. Regrettably, things got nasty between the two groups (Noel Gallagher wishing Damon and Alex death from AIDS being a particular low point) with rancorous ill-feeling remaining for years afterwards.

In the end, 'Country House' beat 'Roll With It' to become Blur's first UK number one single, eventually selling over 600,000 copies. However, the song quickly manifested negative connotations for the band. Despite winning the chart battle, they ultimately lost the war, with Oasis soon eclipsing them in terms of cultural popularity, album sales and – for a while, critical standing. Many would blame 'Country House' for this, with Graham later growing to loathe the track and its 'oompah' connotations. Damon simply attested on *The South Bank Show* in 1999 that it was 'the wrong song for that particular moment'.

Such became the song's stigma that in the immediate years after its release, Blur rarely performed it. But time is a great healer, and since Blur's 2009 reformation, 'Country House' has rightfully reclaimed a regular place in their live set. Though by no means their best work, it's still fondly remembered by fans, and for better or worse, its release was a watershed cultural moment in the band's history.

'Best Days' (Albarn, Coxon, James, Rowntree)

The beautiful and achingly sad 'Best Days' is a perfect example of how adept Damon had become at funnelling his own experiences and emotions into a song that on the surface was about other people – in this instance, commuters ('goodbye to the last train'), taxi drivers ('cabbie has his mind on a fare to the sun') and city businessmen ('in hotel cells listening to dial tones').

Producer Stephen Street was very aware that the song was likely autobiographical in content, telling *Uncut* in 2009:

> I think 'Best Days' pretty accurately sums up how Damon felt at the time – 'All on their own down Soho, take me home' – this is him thinking 'I need to let people know how I feel'. He was weary of it all by now: the fame and the partying.

The track starts with a spooky, reverberated drum loop before Alex and Graham join in, portraying the image of them whisky-soaked, sitting on a porch-front late at night plucking away forlornly in the darkness. Damon's vocal is tender and heartfelt – 'hoping someone is waiting out there' for the passengers leaving London and heading 'out into leafy nowhere'. This melancholy line could be a reflection on his domestic life at the time when he was frequently returning home to an empty flat late at night while his partner Justine Frischmann was away on tour with Elastica. The heartbreaking chorus presumably represents Damon's feelings on Blur's newfound major success and the resulting anguish it unexpectedly brought him:

> Other people wouldn't want to hear you
> If you said that these were the best days of our lives

Other instrumental touches amplifying the song's brokenhearted majesty include Damon's elegiac piano solo (obviously in debt to George Martin's solo on The Beatles' 'In My Life') and Graham's guitar solos – namely the two-part descending scales at 1:39, and the volume pedal swells at 4:26, which give the track a mournful country feel.

A successfully delicate and rare 'Waterloo Sunset'-type moment; if it wasn't for 'The Universal', 'Best Days' may have even been released as the album's big-ballad single.

'Charmless Man' (Albarn, Coxon, James, Rowntree)

A-side single. Released 29 April 1996, UK: 5

This snarky, sniping title could be seen as a reference to The Smiths' 'This Charming Man', though the lyric bears no relation to that tracks' old-fashioned romanticism, and Damon himself has asserted that his song wasn't supposed to be a pun. 'Charmless Man' is the witty yet shallow tale of an upper-class hipster who knows all the 'swingers and their cavalry', 'can get in anywhere for free', but in reality has no discernibly attractive features, and he 'moves in circles of friends who just pretend that they like him'.

The intended target of Damon's lyrical bile has never been clear, though he did tell *Vox Magazine* in 1996: 'It's about clubs like The Groucho and some of the prats you get in there, talking all postmodern about their ad campaigns and the amount of money they make and how great they are. I suppose the song is a little bit about us all as well, especially Alex.'

It's a tightly-constructed and dynamic up-tempo pop-rocker, with a now-commonplace cockney knees-up vocal and an unavoidable 'nah nah nah' earworm of a chorus. Unfortunately, not everyone in the Blur camp was enjoying this new, ultra-pop version of the band. Graham was heavily into bands like Dinosaur Jr. and Pavement at this time, with Stephen Street admitting that nobody involved was catering to him or his tastes. But as he rightly acknowledges, you can't make 'Charmless Man' sound like Pavement.

Ironically, it's Graham's contribution that lifts the track out of its sour and sticky hole. Put simply, his playing is magnificent throughout – spraying virtuosic hammer-on-and-pull-off lead phrases all over the piece, culminating in a fuzzed-out slippery solo that sticks two wonky fingers up at the backing tracks' glossy pop sheen.

Damon later described 'Charmless Man' – the album's fourth and final single – as 'the end of Britpop'. After this single, Blur were to regroup, record the radically different *Blur* LP, and distance themselves totally from this chapter of their career.

And now for some trivia. The verse one reference to infamous East End gangster Ronnie Kray (who died during the making of *The Great Escape*) brought an unexpected surprise when his twin brother Reggie sent Blur a bouquet of flowers for mentioning Ronnie in the lyric.

'Fade Away' (Albarn, Coxon, James, Rowntree)

If there was one word to accurately describe 'Fade Away', it might be 'bleak'. A distinctly two-tone and brass-driven track, it was demoed under the working title of 'Rico' after The Specials' trombonist Rico Rodriguez. The weary-sounding horns suit the mood perfectly, with Alex rather uncharitably claiming that the song is about 'Coventry and Milton Keynes and people with no souls leading empty lives, sort of happily'.

Set to a trudging vocal melody, Damon's lyrics tell the story of a hardworking married couple who have grown apart and now live separate lives. Despite the pair being doomed to a meaningless, hollow existence, they don't seem to care:

> Their birth had been the death of them
> It didn't really bother them
> Now when he's in she's out

It opens with a bossa-nova-type organ intro before the full band enter with a mid-paced and menacing, semi-skanking groove. The performance is hypnotically tight, especially in Graham's chugging verse guitar part, while Dave's snare drum sound and fills are distinctly ska-influenced. Damon adds to the chilly atmosphere with a chromatic piano solo and an eerie three-note organ verse refrain. Underpinning the structure are the chords C and F#m – the Devil's interval (not two-tone but tritone!), an inherent source of the piece's sinister vibes.

The only bit of respite from this all-encompassing gloom comes courtesy of Graham's comedically dark lead guitar chorus touches. Treated with severe vibrato, so the notes wobble uncontrollably, the effect is akin to a smile pulled scarily tight on the face of The Joker.

'Top Man' (Albarn, Coxon, James, Rowntree)

The Great Escape is undoubtedly the poppiest Blur album and is suitably stuffed full of potential singles that never were – 'Top Man' is one of them. Sounding like it took its initial inspiration from Fun Boy Three's 'The Lunatics (Have Taken Over the Asylum)', the arrangement opens with a slightly plodding drum loop that might've been a remnant of Damon's original demo. It's a mid-tempo strut, with Graham's spiky staccato acoustic guitar riff *a la* 'Coping', accompanied by Damon's comedy bass register 'owww' vocals and some whistling straight out of an Ennio Morricone soundtrack.

The lyric describes an oafish wide-boy townie lad ('a little boy racer / Shooting guns on the high street of love'), who may have been modelled on the type of guy that bullied Damon at Stanway Comprehensive back in the 1980s. Like 'Charmless Man', the mood is acridly sarcastic, but also very funny in places, such as this hilarious line:

In a crowd it's hard to spot him
But anonymity can cost
It's never cheap or cheerful
He's Hugo and he's boss

The chorus is a gormless sing-along – 'T-O-P-M-A-N' – a pun on the mainstream high-street clothing brand and a laddish expression to describe a *geezer* or *good bloke*. It calls to mind disco hits of the late-1970s/early-1980s, like 'D.I.S.C.O.' by Ottowan.

Other quirky arrangement details include a tacky middle-eastern keyboard fill over the line 'He's riding through the desert / On a camel lite', while on the following line 'On a magic carpet, he'll fly away tonight', Damon utters a goofy so-bad-it's-good 'open sesame'. Better musical parts are Grahams inventive hanging-in-the-air-like-a-sneeze guitar licks (1.21-1.27) and the descending, slithering off-key arpeggios of the final 'shooting guns' refrain, which portray our brutish protagonist drunkenly stumbling down the saloon steps in some vulgar western-themed fun pub.

'Top Man' is enjoyable, amusing and extremely catchy. It's also crass, trashy and decidedly uncool. Detractors would have had a field day ripping this to shreds if it had been a single.

'The Universal' (Albarn, Coxon, James, Rowntree)

A-side single. Released 13 November 1995. UK: 5

This grandiose masterpiece – *The Great Escape*'s crowning achievement and one of Blur's best-loved singles – was actually conceived during the *Parklife* sessions back in 1993. Demoed in a calypso fashion, 'The Universal' was met with a cool reaction from Graham, who likened it to an early-1990s Lilt commercial (a tropical-fruit soft drink). Damon's girlfriend Justine Frischmann's hostile opinion of the track further crushed his confidence in it; she reportedly detested it. But thankfully, the song had *fans* too. Food's Andy Ross, Stephen Street and Alex all loved it and persuaded Damon to persevere with it. By 1995 they were ready to give it another crack.

But it was here that they ran into problems. Wishing to extricate themselves from the cod-reggae calypso stylings of the 1993 demo (which still hasn't been released), they struggled to find the right drum feel. As Stephen Street explained in *3862 Days*: 'Perhaps because it had once been this weird cod-reggae thing, we couldn't get the rhythm right. I don't know whose idea it was, but we arrived at that big off-beat that seems to push the song along. It's a very odd time signature.'

Alex has since claimed it was Damon who ultimately came up with the correct approach when he composed the now-famous string introduction. The song's rhythm can be compared to a classic 1960s soul ballad, like Ben E. Kings 'Stand by Me' or even Blur's 'Resigned'. What makes it seem unusual is the slowed-down 70 bpm tempo, giving the song an ungainly yet somehow graceful gait.

Once they settled on this off-beat pattern, they recorded the backing track, keeping it sparse and simple in very much the same fashion as 'To the End'. Dave provides a soft backbeat, which Alex sits an easygoing bass line on, embellished occasionally with some three-note runs during vocal breaks, like on 'End of a Century'. Graham is also restrained, playing clean, staccato guitar offbeats, with a delicately-ornate overdubbed second part which in places acts as an answering phrase to the two-note string refrain.

Damon's lyric describes a 21st-century society mollified by The Universal – a government-produced drug modelled on Prozac, resembling Soma from Aldous Huxley's 1931 novel *Brave New World*.

This is the next century
Where the Universal's free
You can find it anywhere
Yes the future's been sold

Verse two describes an Orwellian surveillance state. Today the lyric seems spookily prescient, as the dual state of anaesthesia with mass-monitoring is provided by one omnipresent source: our smartphones.

No one here is alone
Satellites in every home
Yes the Universal's here
Here for everyone

Damon's vocal is affecting, in the same emotional vein as 'To the End'. It's reported that he was anxious to nail the performance, declaring, 'Right, I'm off to make a fool of myself and do my saddo would-be Scott Walker'. It's much like Damon's singing on 'Young and Lovely', and indeed, early-Scott Walker is a clear reference point here. Pulp's Jarvis Cocker – also a Walker fanatic – also comes to mind, especially on the 'every night we're gone' line.

Now all that was needed to send the track into the stratosphere was some orchestration. The Duke String Quartet are arguably the piece's defining feature, while the trumpet after the first chorus is prime Burt Bacharach. Finally, Theresa Davis and Angela Murrell's 'Just let them go' backing vocals add that little bit of fairy dust on top.

Recognised as the album's centrepiece, 'The Universal' was released as the second single. Damon was optimistic, hoping its November release would create an effective contrast against the usual banal Christmas fodder. The single performed well, but was not the smash everyone expected, leaving the top ten after just two weeks.

Today the song is regarded as one of Blur's best singles, often performed live as a glorious showstopping finale. Strangely, since 2009 it's been used in British Gas TV commercials; slightly ironic given the song's darkly-dystopian subject matter.

'Mr Robinson's Quango' (Albarn, Coxon, James, Rowntree)

Just like the song's protagonist, 'Mr Robinsons Quango' is a sleazy tragicomic affair, written at a time in the mid-1990s when sleaze and scandal were rife on the UK political scene. However, unlike 'Tracy Jacks' who was often mistakenly described as a transvestite, the lead character in this bonkers composition was *definitely* a cross-dresser.

Damon recalls that inspiration for the song presented itself when he was on his way to see his grandparents in Grantham. He explained to *NME* in 1995:

> I was at the train station and I wanted to go to the toilet, so I went and sat down, and it had in felt tip on the door – 'I'm wearing black French knickers under my suit, I've got stockings and suspenders on, I'm feeling rather loose', and that's where I took the whole song from.

Developing the lyric from there, it details a high-society mayor-like figure who wears a mason ring, drives an 'expensive car' and attends exclusive events. Incidentally, 'QUANGO' is an acronym for 'Quasi-autonomous non-governmental organisation'. Put simply, it's an institution or company that's partly controlled and/or financed by government bodies, even though most of the government's power regarding said organisation has been delegated elsewhere.

The song debuted live as far back as Blur's Aston Villa Leisure Centre gig on 5 October 1994 and was consequently the first new song recorded for *The Great Escape*. A structurally diverse, sonic whirlpool of a recording, it proved to be the album's most difficult to mix, consisting of at least six contrasting sections, including a filthy, horn-driven funk styled middle eight. Other arrangement highlights are Damon's amusing *Carry On* Kenneth Williams-esque 'Oooh I'm a naughty boy' passage, and Graham's slinky 12-string guitar solo, which has 'spy movie soundtrack' written all over it.

'He Thought of Cars' (Albarn, Coxon, James, Rowntree)

This magnificent and moody track is another album highlight, and at one point, was considered as a possible album finale. As dark as anything Radiohead have produced, the song is a sterile, surrealist news report, conjuring post-apocalyptic images straight out of a J. G. Ballard novel.

Delivered in a bruised and sombre baritone, the verses describe frantic attempts to escape the pressures of the modern world, whilst the damning chorus is a devastating denouement on the protagonist's hopeless position. Delivered in slow motion, the scenes evoke the sensation of trying to run or punch your way out of a disorienting dream.

There's panic at London Heathrow
Everybody wants to go up into the blue
But there's a ten-year queue

He thought of planes
And where, where to fly to
And who to fly there with
But there, there was no one, no one

Much of the peculiar musical atmosphere is so disparate in nature that on paper, it seems ill-fitting. Employing a slow and spooky fade-in (*a la* 'Trouble in the Message Centre'), the track reveals itself as a mushy, mid-paced mooch, driven by Dave's over-compressed drums and Graham's repeated, slippery-'n'-scratchy guitar riff. But when the verses arrive, the mood switches to a soft country shuffle, replete with shaker, bass and lightly-phased acoustic guitar.

Other diverse elements include Damon's quacking-like-a-duck trumpet-synth melody line, and best of all, Grahams clanging, soft rockabilly-style guitar breakdown (played on his 1967 Fender Jag with the all-important tremolo arm), which he proudly likened to Chris Isaak's 1989 classic 'Wicked Game'. Elsewhere, there's spacey *Doctor Who*-style synth lines in verse one, and some queasy, reverse harmonies in the choruses. Praise should also be given to Alex's melody-heavy high chorus bass line.

Though undoubtedly too abstract to be a single, 'He Thought of Cars' is nevertheless a disturbingly-dystopian epic-miniature, proudly displayed on 2009's *Midlife* compilation. With its hazy, almost strung-out detachment, one could argue it was this song that suggested the route Blur would take on their next record, evident on tracks across the board, from 'Beetlebum' to 'Strange News From Another Star'.

'It Could Be You' (Albarn, Coxon, James, Rowntree)

'Heard the neighbour slam his car door / Don't he realise this is respectable street.' Wait, sorry, wrong song! But it does sound like Andy Partridge's band, so much so that during the recording process, 'It Could Be You' – as it was eventually christened – was known as 'The XTC one'. Another outside bet for a UK single (it actually was in Japan), this jerky goof-rocker was recorded in May 1995 and was the album's last recording.

The song began life as a piano ballad called 'Dear Ray', which Damon improvised during a break in rehearsals for his March 1995 appearance on

TV show *The White Room* (where he and Ray Davies sang 'Waterloo Sunset'). During the song's recording, Damon changed the title to 'It Could Be You', which was the recently introduced UK National Lottery's advertising slogan. Obviously angered by the promise to the public of a better life when the odds of winning are roughly 45 million to one, the song bitterly points out what an unrealistic scam the whole thing is.

The chorus lyric is a dichotomy sung from two perspectives – one a pipe-dream of luxury and privilege, and the other a simple existence spent amongst loved ones, which could be argued in reality brings more inner wealth:

All we want is to be happy
In our homes like happy families
Be the man on the beach
With the world at his feet
Yes, it could be you

The verses bring talk of 'telly addicts' (also the name of a 1990s UK TV quiz show hosted by Noel Edmonds), and the controversial line 'Ch-Ch-Ch-Churchil got his lucky number' is a sly dig at Winston Churchill's grandson who accepted £12,000,000 of lottery-funded cash for the sale of the war leader's personal papers.

The track's up-tempo jagged rock displays Graham's rhythmically-taut guitar riffs and spidery arpeggios, while Damon's ultra-cockney vocal is backed up by kooky, dumb-sounding backing vocals – especially in the 'could be meeeeaaay, could be yaaaaouu' breakdown, and the 'don't wuuhhray' part.

'Ernold Same' (Albarn, Coxon, James, Rowntree)

This is the album's waltzing answer to 'The Debt Collector', except this time Damon was able to come up with a short story for its guest narrator: Ken Livingstone. At the time, Livingstone was a popular left-wing MP (eventually London Mayor between 2000 and 2008) who Stephen Street suggested for the role, Livingstone being someone credible with a monotonous voice. Street explained to *NME* in 2021: 'He came in thinking he was the bee's knees and that we were fans – we weren't at all! I couldn't stand him, and my preconceptions were confirmed when he insulted the pastel jumper I was wearing that day!'

In a Ray Davies-esque lyric about a poor sad-sack commuter whose repetitious and tedious life is duplicated *ad nauseam* day-in-day-out, the protagonist is obviously named after Syd Barrett's Pink Floyd character 'Arnold Layne', except Ernold is the opposite of that quirky misfit. Perfectly capturing the lyric's gloomy repetition, Livingstone delivers line after line in a dreary nasal deadpan, before finally sighing 'Poor old Ernold Same'. Damon then comes in singing a sympathetic impassioned vocal, trading off from Livingstone's spoken words, just like he did with Phil Daniels on 'Parklife'.

The intro street noise was captured by hanging a microphone out of Townhouse Studios, thus picking up Goldhawk Road's natural ambience. Damon is audible in the background, shouting comically-garbled obscenities.

Other than the whimsical string section, perhaps the track's most notable arrangement element are Graham's rapid banjo arpeggios, an instrument he impressively learned specifically for the song. Incidentally, a stripped-back version of the song makes a brief reappearance at the end of the album, around 30 seconds after 'Yuko and Hiro' finishes.

'Globe Alone' (Albarn, Coxon, James, Rowntree)

Graham drolly described this rapid, punk-paced track to *Mojo* in 2009: 'It's Damon throwing his toys out of the pram 'cause he can't stand these people in their flash cars who've got the latest mobile phone and are really into hi-fis.'

Indeed, 'Globe Alone' is the tale of a po-faced materialist obsessed with self-image, while the source of his vacuous desires stems from watching TV adverts:

> Who very straight and never grins
> Who cares what car he's driving in
>
> Who wouldn't be seen at bedtime
> Without putting Calvin Kleins on
>
> Because he saw it on a commercial break
> And if he doesn't get what he wants
> Then he gets a headache

The speedy arrangement contains Dave's breakneck double-hi-hat drum pattern, and a nasty distorted Alex bass line, while Graham's spiky guitar riff goes haywire with a brief-but-bonkers atonal solo. Damon's silly and fuzzy synth licks, and Cardiacs-inspired crazy carnival organ add to the dizzy atmosphere.

Enhancing the high-octane energy, Damon's vocal was recorded live with a handheld Shure SM58 microphone, allowing him to leap around the live room as he sang, giving a most raucous performance, and foreshadowing his methods on 'Song 2'.

'Dan Abnormal' (Albarn, Coxon, James, Rowntree)

Not a favourite track of Stephen Street's, the leading man in this scornful character-study is partly – if not wholly – the Blur frontman. Dan Abnormal is an anagram of Damon Albarn. The character is a drunken street yob who assimilates his aggressive way of life from TV programs and movies. Ultimately, the narrator sympathises with the protagonist by declaring him just a product of the modern world:

Meanie Leanie come on down
Come and entertain the town
It's Friday night and we're all bored
Time's been called there is no more
Time's been called it's such a bore

Dan Abnormal not normal at all
It's not his fault we made him this way
He'll imitate you, try to ape you
But it's not his fault Dan watches TV

It was actually Damon's girlfriend Justine who came up with the brilliant moniker, which Damon then brought to life by lending his less-savoury habits to the loutish figure. He explained to the *NME* in 1995: 'The song is about the fact that I spent quite a lot of time on my own, just getting drunk at night. I would find myself in Soho at three in the morning, getting in a taxi and going home to watch a dirty film or something.'

The track is built on a typical vamping Kinks A/G/A/G chord pattern, though David Bowie's 'Aladdin Sane' could've also been an influence – its chorus containing a similar progression and dysfunctional lead character. The motif is mercifully broken during the catchy chorus, with a pretty, bubblegum-flavoured melody over the F#/D/B7/E chord sequence.

Other notable touches include the schticky falsetto 'la la la la''s, and the 'TV' (pronounced 'Tay-Vay') sections after each chorus, a quotation of sorts from Wire's 'Ex Lion Tamer' from their *Pink Flag* LP. Graham's guitar contribution is not so pivotal on this occasion, though he does nail an impressively unhinged Dave Davies-esque guitar solo after the 'Give us it' middle eight.

'Entertain Me' (Albarn, Coxon, James, Rowntree)

This was one of the earliest songs demoed for the album, under the working title 'Bored Housewives'. Listening to that early draft, you can hear many elements that made it to the final version (Sadly, the vocoder idea was dumped), including Graham's feedback-drenched chords and his Blondie-esque 'Atomic' post-chorus lick.

Also taking shape nicely on the demo was Alex's snaking bass line, presumably inspired by Gary Numan's 'We Take Mystery (to Bed)'. At the time, Damon described Alex's bass part as 'his best in years', conveniently forgetting his funky contribution to 'Girls & Boys', which was very similar. Stephen Street spoke of Alex's undeniable talent in *3862 Days*: 'He's completely fantastic, but he'll sit next to me in the control room and fire off all these different bass lines. You've got to say, 'That bit there'.'

Like 'Girls & Boys', the song is built on one persistent chord sequence, with the instrumentation tightly metronomic in order to contrast with the grooving bass pulse. Dave's ringing drums are looped but for the occasional decoration, while underneath, Damon's chugging sequenced synthesizer part glues the arrangement together, appearing most prevalently in the introduction.

In the verses, Damon does a decent impression of The Fall's Mark E. Smith – the semi-distorted drawl speak-singing its way around lyrics describing a weekend ritual of going to the football ('Head to the floodlights, see the fraternity'), while verse two deals with the anxiety and expectations of entertaining a date:

She wants a loose fit
He wants instant whip
Guesstimates her arrival
But will she want it, really badly

Like so many 1990s indie-dance anthems, the chorus is a big, loud, catchy chant of the song title, but unlike those often warmhearted paeans to togetherness, this track has a cold, detached atmosphere, thus rendering it unsuitable for single-release.

'Yuko and Hiro' (Albarn, Coxon, James, Rowntree)
This has the distinction of being the album's only love song, but this alone doesn't make the recording unique. Being a peculiarly innovative production in which the Far East and outer space collide, the track was Damon's favourite when it was released, claiming he'd never heard a song like it.

It begins with a 'Lot 105'-type built-in organ drum rhythm, sampled and chopped up to form a completely original pattern. Graham's otherworldly guitar lines come in over the top. Fractured, pitch-shifted and heavily-phased, they give an impression of semi-molten metal buckling under extreme heat.

Damon's verse vocal appears to be artificially double-tracked, while chorus two's delay on the word 'forever' (akin to Alex's voice at the end of 'Far Out') portrays a lonely astronaut floating through the cosmos into infinity.

Talking of being lonely, the song is a heartbreaking tale sung from the perspective of Hiro – a company employee who rarely gets to see his girlfriend due to the monopoly both of their jobs have over their time. Originally titled 'Japanese Workers', Stephen Street could tell it was a thinly-veiled attempt on Damon's part to articulate the sorrow felt in his own love life, and the strain that two careers in the pop industry were placing on it. Street told *Uncut* in 2009: 'As soon as we started working on it, I said to Damon, 'It's about you and Justine, isn't it?' It's very poignant, which is why I suggested it should be the final track on the album.'

The presence of a foreign female counter-lead-vocal, coupled with the lovesick subject matter, made the track an obvious candidate for the album's answer to 'To the End'. To play the role of Yuko, Damon wanted an authentic Japanese-style vocalist, not 'some Japanese rock chick'. Threatened with the possibility of Damon using a cassette sample from Portobello Market, Stephen

Street brought in Cathy Gillat, who provided two voices – one spoken, one sung – roughly translating the lyrics into Japanese.

Easily one of the album's most underappreciated songs, 'Yuko and Hiro' is a decidedly sad and strange way to end this decidedly sad and strange pop album.

Contemporary Tracks

'One Born Every Minute' (Albarn, Coxon, James, Rowntree)

B-side to 'Country House'

Described by Damon as 'The Kinks song Ray Davies never wrote', this is a jaunty, cockney knees-up that was penned at the same Christmas 1992 writing session that produced 'For Tomorrow'. Demoed with John Smith at Matrix in mid-1993, the original backing track of drums, bass, organ and guitars was kept for the final released version, with Graham's opening lick sounding not unlike the theme from *The Addams Family*. Much later, Damon recorded new and improved double-tracked vocals, backing vocals and piano, with an array of comedic sound effects including kazoo, bicycle horns and a bird whistle.

A rousing celebration of the hedonistic side of (pop) life, the opening sing-along lyrics could be seen by many as an entry in Alex James' tour diary circa 1995:

> Here we go again, here we go again
> Dirty knickers, pop music, vodka and gin

The irony is that the band have never performed the song live. Nevertheless, due to its position as the only new composition featured on the mega-selling 'Country House' single, the song is one of Blur's best-known B-sides, and despite the jovial 'Yellow Submarine'-type atmosphere, is a deceptively strong composition.

'Ultranol' (Albarn, Coxon, James, Rowntree)

B-side to 'The Universal'

This is a Stephen Street-produced outtake from the *Great Escape* sessions, and opens with Madness-type piano, before settling into a Kinks 'Plastic Man' stomp. It's basically a musical advert for a fictitious magic lozenge ('Suck 'em and see') – a wonder drug that cures all ailments from 'funny turns and Chinese burns' to 'aches and pains and jellied brains'; even claiming to 'revitalise that sexual drive'.

Damon's lyric is well-crafted, and the arrangement is tight and lively, featuring a catchy – if silly – falsetto 'n-n-n-na' hook and Graham's quirky guitar embellishments. Damon later wrote a similar piece as the theme tune to the short-lived 1997 UK sitcom *Sunnyside Farm*, which starred Phil Daniels.

'No Monsters in Me' (Albarn, Coxon, James, Rowntree)

B-side to 'The Universal'

This faintly-menacing rocker was another Stephen Street-produced outtake, and featured as the last track on the album's Japanese edition. Creeping up with an eerie one-note keyboard drone, the track lurches along on Graham's propulsive heavy metal-ish octave guitar riff, while Dave keeps time with a hard, hi-hat-heavy rhythm like 'Oily Water' on speed.

The superbly surreal lyric concerns a character called Gary Golf who reads Dick Francis novels 'In Dazzed pyjamas and sheets' (Daz is a British washing powder) while car alarms 'let off steam' in his sleep. The distinctly non-melodic verses do not alleviate the song's obtuse nature, though the poppy 'na na na na na' chorus *is* naggingly addictive.

'The Man Who Left Himself' (Albarn, Coxon, James, Rowntree)

B-side to 'Stereotypes'

In January 1996, Blur returned to the studio with John Smith to record B-sides for *The Great Escape*'s remaining singles. This song – along with 'Tame' – clearly indicates the elements that would define the next album – looser performances and arrangements, hazier soundscapes, and the introduction of lazier, less cockney-geezer-type vocals.

Taking a cue from Morrissey's 'Seasick, Yet Still Docked', 'The Man Who Left Himself' is a slow, bluesy, country shuffle with sloppy handclaps, sounding like a downtrodden, introspective early take on 'Tender'. The oblique lyric describes people that work forever to the point that they become invisible and, therefore, leave their body.

Though never performed live, Damon did dig the song out for a 2014 solo gig at the Royal Albert Hall, prompting a guest appearance from Graham, who unleashed a thrilling and wild guitar solo towards the song's close.

'Tame' (Albarn, Coxon, James, Rowntree)

B-side to 'Stereotypes'

This sturdy grunge-rocker was another clue to the direction Blur's fifth LP would take. Opening on Graham's ominous and tricky guitar riff (with a dark tone similar to 'Wear Me Down'), 'Tame' is built around a circling four-chord sequence of ascending minor-3rd's (C#m/ E/G/Bb), with the band jamming a ghostly mid-paced groove, and sharp synths slicing through the mix.

Damon's mysterious stream-of-consciousness verse lyrics talk of 'clear skies', 'aeroplanes passing at a slight angle', 'coffee mornings' and 'show bonanzas', while the chorus offers a telling glimpse into his post-Britpop war psyche:

I don't know what to do
The day is up to you
Can I pass through you?

It's a moment of despair and unease not heard since 1992, and the repeated falsetto song title refrain hits home a word later used to describe his life's work in 'Strange News From Another Star'.

'Ludwig' (Albarn, Coxon, James, Rowntree)
B-side to 'Stereotypes'

Aside from melodic humming, some 'ay-ya-ya-ya' and a megaphone-shouted 'And all's good!', 'Ludwig' is a wordless Mariachi-band-meets-ska-calypso piece that sounds like it was written and recorded in about 30 minutes. Quite possibly named after the make of drum kit Dave was playing at the time, the recording is a good-natured, pleasant piece of throwaway fluff that would've been perfect for an El Paso Taco commercial.

'The Horrors' (Albarn, Coxon, James, Rowntree)
B-side to 'Charmless Man'

This solo-Damon four-track demo is a wonderfully melancholic Erik Satie-esque instrumental and a moment of pure unadulterated musical inspiration. Structured in two sections, the piece is a fine example of the singer's gift for melody and knack for interesting chord sequences. It also has a fair amount in common with Damon's solo track 'Closet Romantic' (which – alongside 'Sing' – featured on the *Trainspotting* soundtrack), in that it features a similar accompaniment to the 'Lot 105' organ and wordless vocals, giving the impression that both were composed for submission, and 'Closet Romantic' was the chosen piece.

'A Song' (Albarn, Coxon, James, Rowntree)
B-side to 'Charmless Man'

Another Damon demo, you could see this as an exercise in record label barrel-scraping. But it's still a fascinating curio, giving a drowsily-intimate glimpse inside Damon's writing process, with a lyric that appears to offer a critical look at the effect TV culture has on social interaction:

When he speaks to her
Without looking at her
Using the driest of words
With his mind on what's on the telly

Incidentally, Damon performed 'A Song' at the 7 July 1996 Poetry Olympics at The Royal Albert Hall. It also marks his first composition with the word 'song' in the title – something he'd frequently do in the future with 'Song 2', 'Woodpigeon Song', 'Mellow Song', 'Good Song' and 'Sweet Song'.

'St Louis' (Albarn, Coxon, James, Rowntree)

B-side to 'Charmless Man'

On 7 February 1996, Blur played a show at The Galaxy Club in St Louis, and if the lyrics of this song are anything to go by, they didn't want to be there. Recorded during two months of solid stateside touring, 'St Louis' is a pretty, melodic 1960s-type pop track that's marred by poor audio quality, giving the impression that the song was cut in a weary, hurried haze. It's a shame because it's a decent sad-on-the-road kind of song that perhaps deserved more care and attention. Rumour has it that Damon and Graham had a huge row during the recording, suggesting that the band were burning out and severely needed a rest.

'Eine Kleine Lift Musik' (Albarn, Coxon, James, Rowntree)

Released on War Child's The Help Album, 9 September 1995

This was Blur's contribution to *The Help Album* – a charity record to raise funds for the War Child Charity, which provided aid to war-stricken areas such as Bosnia and Herzegovina. Also including Radiohead, Oasis and Paul McCartney, all the songs were recorded on Monday 4 September 1995.

This whimsical piece in 12/8 is like a faster, sunnier version of The Righteous Brothers' 'Unchained Melody'. Featuring a badly-out-of-tune lead piano, this virtually wordless track was originally recorded as a demo called 'Hope You Find Your Suburbs'. It contained a lead vocal with the 'wife swapping is your future' line (which was later used in 'Stereotypes'), and if Damon had completed the words, it would've brought welcome light-relief to *The Great Escape* after the heartbreak of 'Yuko and Hiro', bringing the album full-circle and adding to its inherent West End-musical quality.

Blur (1997)

Personnel:
Damon Albarn: Lead vocals, Piano, Keyboards, Hammond organ, Acoustic guitar
Graham Coxon: Guitars, Backing vocals, Vocal on 'You're So Great', Theremin, Additional drums on 'Song 2' and 'Strange News from Another Star'
Alex James: Bass
Dave Rowntree: Drums, Percussion, Programming on 'On Your Own'
Recorded: June-November 1996 at Maison Rouge, Mayfair and 13 (London); Studio Grettisgat, Reykjavik
Producers: Stephen Street, Blur
Release dates: UK: 10 February 1997, US: 11 March 1997
Label: Food/Parlophone (UK), Virgin (US)
Chart Placings: UK: 1, US: 61

In the aftermath of the brutal Britpop war with Oasis, Blur found themselves battered, defeated and on the verge of implosion. Graham, in particular, had grown to loathe his job as 'guitarist from Blur', and the incessant touring demands of being a top draw act; he was now at loggerheads with the rest of the group and their polished pop sound. Damon was also in an extreme state of anguish. In early 1996 – weary of fame, and tortured by public reaction swinging viciously against him and the band – he began writing introspective new material, unsure whether there would even be another Blur record.

Stephen Street was given the tricky task of talking Graham around – a tactic that paid off when the troubled guitarist wrote Damon a letter saying he wanted to musically 'scare people' again. An olive branch offering of sorts, it was agreed by all that Graham would be given a much freer hand to express himself on LP five, with the orchestral and arrangement excesses of *The Great Escape* drastically pared back.

The recording location was another hurdle. Damon – seeking solace from the pressures of London – had recently spent time rejuvenating in Iceland, and wanted to record the album in Reykjavik. In desperate need of stability after a gruelling few years on the road, Graham was vehemently against the idea and insisted on recording in London. A compromise was struck – the band would lay down the bulk of instrumentation at Mayfair Studios in Primrose Hill (close to Graham's newly-purchased Camden home), and Stephen Street and Damon would then travel to Iceland to record the vocals.

Following two weeks of relaxed jamming at John Henry's rehearsal studios, sessions proper began at Mayfair in June 1996 and continued intermittently over the following months. For all intents and purposes, the band fractures were healed, with the guys enjoying the process of creating their earthy new recordings.

Released in February 1997, the new album was simply called *Blur* – Graham describing the title as a reevaluation of what the band name meant. Heralding a radical change in direction, the record incorporated dub, grunge and lo-fi influences, while fashionable US alt-rock luminaries Beck, Pavement and Tortoise were name-checked in interviews. Ironically, by forgoing the shiny pop of yore and producing a looser sound less concerned with commercial expectations, *Blur* became their biggest-selling album worldwide. Propelled by the unprecedented success of 'Song 2', it even went gold in the US: selling in excess of 600,000 units. Equally significant was the impact it had on the group and their critical standing – seen by the UK music press as a courageous and exciting about-face, it proved the band still had plenty to offer creatively. In other words, *Blur* saved Blur's bacon.

'Beetlebum' (Albarn, Coxon, James, Rowntree)

A-side single. Released 20 January 1997. UK:1

Blur's first post-Britpop single can be seen as another aesthetic and artistic rebirth, in much the same way that 'For Tomorrow' had been three years previously. This time, a soft, languid vocal delivery and a personal narrative replaced the third-person character studies and chipper estuary-English, while the band's no-frills back-to-basics arrangement showcased a newfound maturity and depth of emotion. With 'Beetlebum', Blur were really feeling the music.

In a 1996 MTV interview, Damon explained that the title was a word describing a feeling he was accustomed to that was 'sort of sleepy and sort of sexy', while simultaneously admitting he wasn't quite sure *what* it meant. However, it seems the word's origin may stem from a 1948 Spike Jones and His City Slickers song called 'William Tell Overture', which repeatedly says the word 'Beetlebaum'. Graham has since asserted that when they were young, he and Damon would listen to it 'in a slightly altered state, and giggle'.

As for the song's meaning, Damon has revealed it is indeed about his heroin experience with girlfriend Justine Frischmann. Damon assumed he was being quite transparent when he wrote the lyric, and was surprised when no one cottoned on. We can now presume the title to be a drug terminology reference, deriving from the black dotted residue left on tin foil sheets after heroin use, often called beetles, hence the phrase 'chasing the beetle'.

Of course, 'beetle' is also an astute play on the notion that the song itself is a class-A *White Album*-era Beatles tribute. The double-tracked falsetto chorus vocal is cut from the same dreamy cloth as the 'I don't know why' sections in George Harrison's 'While My Guitar Gently Weeps', and Damon's strung-out verse vocal has a lot in common with 'Happiness Is a Warm Gun' and Lennon's solo track 'Hold On'. Accordingly, Damon told *NME* at the time: 'I want Noel (Gallagher) to listen to 'Beetlebum' and realise that this is closer (to the Beatles).' Serendipitously, Gallagher has duly cited 'Beetlebum' as his favourite Damon composition.

The expansive backing track opens with one of Graham's most famous guitar riffs – a quick slide-up and three power-chord downstrokes that the scratchy demo's offbeat drum pattern may have inspired. The beat emphasis on this riffy rhythm seems confusing, and Graham has since admitted that they often messed this up in live shows, but if you count four-to-the-bar from the very beginning, it plays straight through.

Other notable elements include a superb serpentine bassline, and Graham's looping Hank Marvin-esque guitar line in the coda. There's also a plethora of unnerving sound effects at 4:20 – likely the result of Damon uttering bizarre vocals into a Dictaphone; you can hear its stop button being clicked at the end.

With the basic track completed at Mayfair in early June 1996, Damon and Stephen Street (with Alex along for the ride) immediately flew to Iceland to work on the vocals. Footage of these sessions has emerged online – an Icelandic news report shows Damon recording these heartfelt and wearied vocals in an England football shirt. The report states that this was the day England faced Holland in Euro '96, meaning the vocal session's precise date would be 18 June 1996.

At this point, the vocals were complete, and a tearfully-awed Stephen Street realised he had something special on his hands. But upon the single's January 1997 release, there was concern over its chart prospects, with media talk of the song's moody, pensive tone being akin to commercial suicide. They needn't have worried, as a positive critical reception and Blur's now-massive hardcore fan base ensured that 'Beetlebum' shot straight to number 1 in the UK – the first chart-topper there ever to be recorded in Iceland – building anticipation for the soon-to-be-released *Blur* album.

Since the single's release, the song has featured in all major live sets, and was chosen to open 2000's *Blur: Best Of* compilation, with Street rightly assessing the song to be one of the pinnacles of Blur's catalogue.

'Song 2' (Albarn, Coxon, James, Rowntree)

A-side single. Released 7 April 1997. UK: 2, US Alt-rock: 6, US Main Rock: 25

The irony with 'Song 2' – Blur's best-known song and their biggest money-spinner – is that it was recorded as a bit of throwaway fun when they were waiting for some studio equipment to arrive. Damon has even said it was a complete afterthought for inclusion on the album.

One of the key elements in its creation was Stephen Street's new digital hard-disk recording device: the Otari RADAR – capable of recording and playing up to 24 tracks of 16-bit 48k audio. In a recording lull, Graham and Dave's simultaneously played the opening drum loop – the two jamming a rhythm on two drum kits set up for contrasting songs. One kit was set up in the reflective-reverb end of the studio, the other end with a much more dead sound. Also, the drums were not close mic'ed, but simply recorded using room-ambience mics.

The drum pattern itself was a straightforward 4/4 rock beat, Graham joining in with a looser feel, striking the rims instead of the hi-hat with the occasional tom hit. Street's ears pricked up and he captured the duelling drummers on his new machine, looping eight bars in the process. Realising the loop had something, the guys decided to overdub an interpretation of a slow acoustic Damon demo that contained a wolf-whistle chorus. The rest is history.

Completed in one afternoon, the resulting track was a triumph of feeling-over-meaning. Graham's guitar introduced the famous five-chord riff, which he performed on a Telecaster with his Marshall stack turned down. Once the chorus explodes with Dave's cymbal-heavy hard-rock rhythm, Alex's distorted bass comes to the fore, setting the sonic landscape ablaze; he later revealed it was achieved with a homemade distortion box. It's also one of two bass parts in the arrangement, as he plays the two-note sliding hook over the top in the post-chorus section and again during the ending sequence. Graham speculated that this was likely played through a tiny, battery-powered Marshall amp.

Damon's memorable vocal was mainly a guide track he laid down using an SM57 in the control room, sung simultaneously with the band playing. A listen to the vocal-only stem confirms this, revealing lots of control-room sound bleed. Incidentally, the song made its live debut at the Hultsfred Festival in Sweden on 15 June 1996, just days after the track was recorded, and Damon was evidently not convinced by his vocals. Singing lyrics at random, he confessed on stage, 'I don't know what it's called and I don't know what it's about 'cause I haven't really written it yet'. Stephen Street asserts that they tried re-recording the vocal later with different lyrics, but it didn't work, and Damon eventually simply doubled the chorus with a condenser mic, for added power.

The nonsense made-up-on-the-spot lyrics are the key to the song's innate genius. Lines like, 'I got my head checked by a jumbo jet' and 'When I feel heavy metal, and I'm pins and I'm needles' are so oblique, they render the song meaningless and yet somehow universal.

With the track complete, the band had no idea it would even *be* on the album they were making, let alone be a single, as Graham recalled to *Produce Like a Pro* in 2019: 'The label came into the studio and we played it to them giggling, saying 'Lets play them that one', as a joke to scare them. But they said, 'That's a single!', so our joke was foiled.'

Eventually released as the album's second single, the two-minute-long 'Song 2' shot to number 2 in the UK and was a hit all over the world – including the USA where it landed Blur with the slightly-unwanted tag 'The woo-hoo guys'. More significant than any chart position, though, was the track's use in media worldwide – usually to accompany images of things moving extremely fast or to demonstrate a state of carefree abandon. A month before the single's release, US computer hardware behemoths Intel released their Pentium 2 processor, using 'Song 2' in its ad campaign. This opened the floodgates to unprecedented exposure, ranging from TV ads to movies, programs, video games and sports arenas – you name it, they used it. Incredibly, the US army (Northrop Grumman) wanted to use it as theme music for video packages unveiling their new stealth bomber. They were reportedly offering phenomenal amounts of cash, but the band declined.

'Song 2' is almost single-handedly responsible for *Blur* being the band's best-selling LP. It's without doubt Blur's most widely-known piece of music, currently out-streaming its nearest competitor 'Girls & Boys' on Spotify at a ratio of 4:1 (almost 400,000,000 streams at the time of writing). No live Blur show is complete without 'Song 2', and in just two years following its original release, it earned them over £2,000,000. Today, that amount has more than likely tripled – not bad for a song that was recorded in under an hour and that many described as a grunge parody.

'Country Sad Ballad Man' (Albarn, Coxon, James, Rowntree)
On the run-up to the album release, Damon stated that one of his biggest writing inspirations in this period was US artist Beck, and it's perhaps on this song that his influence is most prevalent.

The track opens with the unusual combo of Jew's harp and guitar-string scratching before a slow brushes groove enters. The song starts proper with Graham's acoustic guitar intro, followed by Alex on double bass: a first on a Blur recording. The overall effect is wonky and porch-front primitive, not dissimilar to the 'Best Days' intro, but with an earthier authenticity. It's at this point that one thinks of Beck – more specifically, the track 'Pay No Mind (Snoozer)' from his 1994 *Mellow Gold* LP – while the double bass gives off a certain countrified Rolling Stones 'Sweet Virginia' flavour.

Damon's distorted lo-fi lead vocal (recorded through a guitar amp) spits out partly autobiographical lyrics dealing with his fear of becoming washed-up after the media backlash that followed *The Great Escape*:

Yeah I found nowhere
It got to know me
Let me sleep all day
Spent the money

VIP 223
Had my chances
And they had me

He also found inspiration in the story of American singer P. J. Proby. Having had a number of UK pop hits in the 1960s, Proby disappeared from public view, spending obscure years living in a mobile home in Northamptonshire, having spent the money he earned from his early success.

Graham's charmingly ramshackle guitar solo was played on the same Fender Musicmaster featured in the 'Beetlebum' video. It was recorded in one take, a placeholder performance mapping out the solo's structure, that was kept. Then comes the Pavement-esque hard-rocking outro sequence, with a wobbly, vibrato-heavy breakdown that sounds like he'd been listening to 'Peaches' by The Presidents of The United States of America. Not surprisingly, Graham was a big fan of 'Country Sad Ballad Man', professing in *3862 Days*: 'It has a quality to the sound that makes me feel good. The real organicness of it, the fact that the bass and the guitar are so far out of tune from each other. That makes me quite happy.'

'M.O.R' (Albarn, Coxon, James, Rowntree, Bowie, Eno)

A-side single. Released 15 September 1997. UK: 15

This 1970's glam/art-rock inspired track was another Damon wrote in response to the recent downturn in Blur's popularity and hipness. Lines like 'Fall into fashion, fall out again' confirm this, while the fraternal sentiments behind 'We stick together' and 'We'll work it out' are a reference to their interpersonal struggles over the past year or so and the determination to see it through, because 'It never ends'. The title acronym (for middle of the road) is perhaps a comment on where Blur's music had sometimes veered dangerously towards during the *Great Escape* period.

From the beginning, Graham is given free rein to dominate the arrangement, opening with an aggressive D-note octave lick that boasts a brilliantly fast and precise tremolo effect on the ascending slide at the end of the four-bar sequence. Elsewhere, his playing is wild and ferocious before leading the band into a crazy, frenetic stupor at the song's close.

Around the time of release, Damon claimed that the characteristic call-and-response vocals were influenced by Roxy Music; though, unfortunately for him, David Bowie's lawyers had other ideas, rightly pointing out that they were in fact, very close to the chorus of Bowie's 'Boys Keep Swinging'. This and the fact that the D/A/Bb verse chord sequence was also identical to Bowie's 'Fantastic Voyage' (both Bowie songs from 1979's *Lodger*) meant that the band had little choice but to include Bowie and Brian Eno in the songwriting credits.

Released as the album's fourth and final single, 'M.O.R.' landed in the UK chart at a disappointing 15: the lowest chart entry in their homeland since 'End of a Century' three years previous. Though the band recorded a new and even more raucous 'Road Version' of the track (with Graham on backing vocals) while on tour in Japan, that frustratingly didn't feature on the UK release despite being titled 'M.O.R. – Road Version'. Alex also claims the single's relative failure was down to the one CD-only format (as opposed to two), lamenting, 'It got to number shit as a result'.

Easily one of Blur's most overlooked mid-period singles, 'M.O.R.' – like 'Stereotypes' – was omitted from 2000's *Blur: The Best Of* compilation and was not performed in any of their big come back shows in 2009, 2012 or 2015.

'On Your Own' (Albarn, Coxon, James, Rowntree)

A-side single. Released 16 June 1997. UK: 5.

In recent years, Damon has referred to 'On Your Own' as one of the first-ever Gorillaz tunes. With its languid electronic rhythm, a half-sung/half-rapped vocal

Top: A young Blur, around the time of *Leisure*'s release in 1991.

Above: Checking out the Blur special supplement in the Grimsby Telegraph, September 1995.

Left: *Leisure* (1991). The debut album's cover photo was taken in 1954 for a *Picture Post* fashion feature on bathing hats. (*Food*)

Right: Graham and Damon look to the future in the promo for 'Bang', 1991.

Left: Damon in the video for 'There's No Other Way', 1991. That bowl cut was soon for the chopping block.

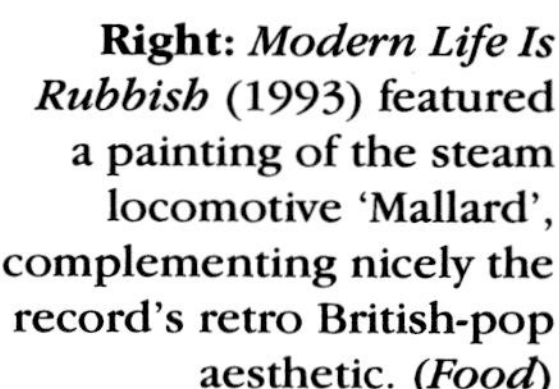

Right: *Modern Life Is Rubbish* (1993) featured a painting of the steam locomotive 'Mallard', complementing nicely the record's retro British-pop aesthetic. *(Food)*

Left: A youthful-looking Dave in the 'Chemical World' promo, 1993.

Right: Alex relaxing and enjoying nature in the 'Chemical World' video, 1993.

Left: *Parklife* (1994). The iconic dog racing shot for Blur's epochal third album was taken in Essex, at Romford Greyhound Stadium. (*Food*)

Right: Actor Phil Daniels enjoys a 'cuppa' in the 'Parklife' promo, 1994.

Left: The comedic 'Parklife' video was shot next door to the Pilot Inn pub in Greenwich, London.

This page: Images from the 'To The End' promo, 1994. Filmed in Prague, the video was inspired by the 1961 French New Wave movie *Last Year At Marienbad.*

Left: *The Great Escape* (1995). An idealist's fantasy of a cover that belied the sarcastically dark pop within. (*Food*)

Right: Actor Keith Allen takes a bath in the Damien Hirst directed 'Country House' promo, 1995.

Left: Alex reading some Balzac in the 'Country House' video, 1995.

Right: Channelling their inner Queen during the 'blow, blow me out' breakdown section of 'Country House', 1995.

Left: The Blur vs Oasis chart battle was the biggest national talking point in Britain during the summer of 1995.

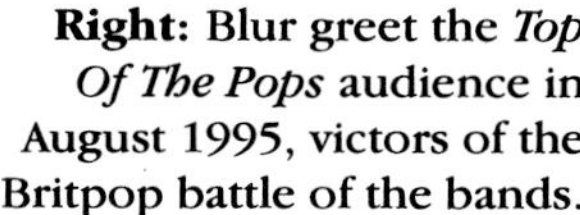

Right: Blur greet the *Top Of The Pops* audience in August 1995, victors of the Britpop battle of the bands.

Left: *A Clockwork Orange* inspired the video for 'The Universal', featuring the band dressed up like Droogs, 1995.

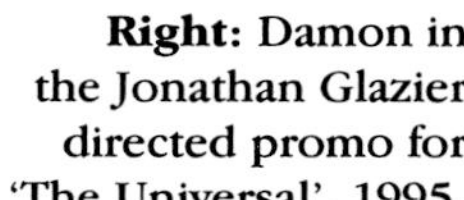

Right: Damon in the Jonathan Glazier directed promo for 'The Universal', 1995.

Left: Damon about to be thrown to the ground in the 'Charmless Man' video, 1996.

Right: This woozy hospital scene aptly visualises what a career-saving album *Blur* (1997) turned out to be. (*Food*)

Left: The back-to-basics, rehearsal room video for 'Beetlebum', 1997.

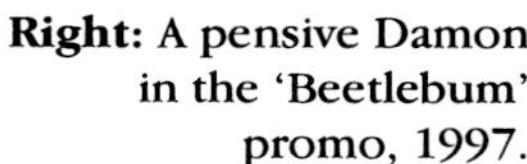

Right: A pensive Damon in the 'Beetlebum' promo, 1997.

Left: The experimental *13* (1999) featured an oil painting by Graham called *Apprentice* on its cover. (*Food*)

Right: Dave prepares himself to be filmed in bed. 'No Distance Left To Run' promo, 1999.

Left: Graham interviewed in the 'No Distance Left To Run' video (1999), a film which documented the band as they slept.

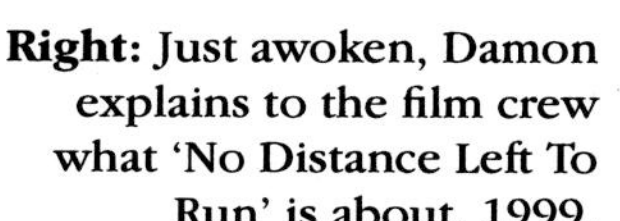

Right: Just awoken, Damon explains to the film crew what 'No Distance Left To Run' is about, 1999.

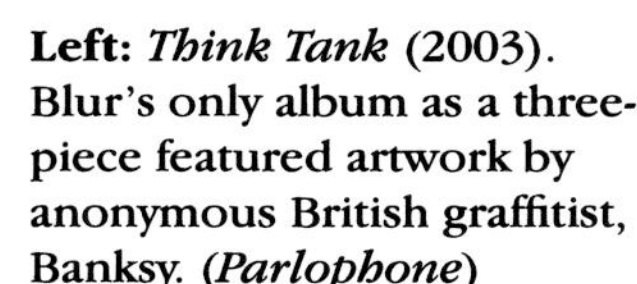

Left: *Think Tank* (2003). Blur's only album as a three-piece featured artwork by anonymous British graffitist, Banksy. (*Parlophone*)

Right: And then there were three. The promo for 'Crazy Beat', 2003.

This page: Shots from the 2012 Brit Awards, where Blur were honoured with the 'Outstanding Contribution to Music' gong.

This page: Blur at the Brit awards in 2012. In a short 'greatest hits' set, the band played 'Girls and Boys', 'Song 2' and 'Parklife'.

This page: In 2015, Blur performed in Hong Kong, where they recorded their eighth studio album, *The Magic Whip*. (*Parlophone*)

This page: More shots from the band's 2015 concert in Hong Kong.

Left: ***The Magic Whip*** **(2015). Blur's final album? The neon-lit cover was designed by Hong Kong artist Tony Hung.**

Above: Britpop's elder statesmen, photographed in 2015.

– not to mention a simplistic three-chord sequence – you can see his point. Whether the rest of the band would agree with this statement is debatable, but what *is* accepted is the fact it was one of the first demos made for the *Blur* LP.

Graham's opening riff is a quintessential example of his particular genius – a rapid hammer-on-and-off on the third string, followed by a quick three-note lick and an F# power chord. The most intriguing aspect is the juddering, drill-like sound effect at the end of the phrase – achieved by setting a Boss delay pedal to a short delay time with plenty of feedback while making a non-musical sound on the guitar.

Dave programmed the drum pattern with a Roland TR-606 Drumatix: a 1980s drum machine. This now-vintage piece of kit can be seen in the song's music video, which shows Dave performing perched inside a hole in the ground. Another notable rhythm track element is Alex's hooky three-note high-descending and low-ascending bass runs in the post-chorus sections.

The verses are from the Bob Dylan school of speak-singing, and you could just imagine Mr Zimmerman singing these lines:

Holy man tip-toed his way across the Ganges
The sound of magic music in his ears
Videoed by a bus load of tourists
Shiny shell suits on and drinking lemonade

The anthemic chorus is even less melodic – a Happy Mondays-esque one-note chant designed for a beery sing-along with arms around your mates down the pub. It's not too dissimilar a vibe to Chumbawamba's 1997 hit 'Tubthumping', except the slightly esoteric lyrics 'I'll eat parole, dig gold card soul' are perhaps too tricky to remember on a drunken Saturday night.

Nevertheless, when released as the album's third single, 'On Your Own' managed a number-5 UK chart placing, no doubt aided by a live rendition of 'Popcene' being included as one of the B-sides. It was the first time the song had been available on CD since its original 1992 single release, making it a desirable purchase for die-hard fans.

'Theme From Retro' (Albarn, Coxon, James, Rowntree)

Fading in on an ominous detuned guitar twang, 'Theme From Retro' was the most abstruse recording Blur had ever placed on an LP up to this point and would've surely confounded many fans who'd come on board with the previous two albums. This delirious organ-driven old-time swing track conjures ghostly images of a World War II dance band performing in an empty palais, oblivious to the building burning down around them.

It seems that the most likely inspiration behind this disorienting piece was The Specials – especially tracks like 'Man At C&A' and 'International Jet Set' (both from 1980's *More Specials),* which feature a similar spooky minor ambience and unusual vocal textures. However, on 'Theme From Retro', Blur push the sound boundaries further into chaos and noise, with indecipherable dubby vocals and distorted guitar textures creating a nightmarish scenario. Meanwhile, Alex's double bass and Dave's heavily compressed and reverberated drums shuffle away breezily in the hazy distance.

The mangled and distorted voice that appears at the end (played at half speed then sped up again at 3:24) is actually a doorman from a US nightclub the group visited on tour. Referring to the tape machine itself, he clearly says, 'Uh-oh, what is that device right there?'.

'You're So Great' (Coxon)

Grahams first (and currently last) solo composition to feature on a Blur album was written when he temporarily gave up alcohol after the June 1996 concert in Dublin. Recounted by its writer as 'Me filling in some time on an afternoon', 'You're So Great' was written in a period of sobriety while listening to the Big Star LP *Sister Lovers.*

Presented to the band as a dictaphone demo, Stephen Street was an early champion of the song and wanted to record it as soon as he heard it. With an embarrassed Graham sitting beneath a table in the darkened studio, he and Street sought to recreate the demo's ramshackle charm and even overdubbed record scratches, giving the track a lo-fi ambience akin to a 78-rpm gramophone record. Like his lyrics on 'Coffee & TV', the song is a frank description of Graham's struggle with alcohol, and his reliance on caffeine to get him through.

Sad, drunk and poorly
Sleep in really late
Sad, drunk and poorly
Not feeling so great

Tea, tea and coffee,
Helps to start the day
DT and Coffee
Shakin' all the way

Street has praised the wounded slide guitar break, calling it 'pure George Harrison', with Graham happily acknowledging the Beatles guitarist as a huge influence on his playing overall.

Despite its rugged, rickety approach, 'You're So Great' is a genuinely heartfelt addition to *Blur,* possessing a vulnerability and universality that could've made the track an intriguing option as a single. Indeed, it's the album's fourth-highest streamed Spotify song – not far behind 'On Your Own' (which has the advantage of featuring on 2000's *Blur: The Best Of*). It also holds the distinction of being the only Blur album track with no other Blur members playing on it ('Optigan I' at least has samples of other musicians on it). Feeling that Grahams lone, fragile voice had a plaintive quality, Stephen Street made the decision to not include anyone else, saying, 'I just wanted Graham to have that moment for himself'.

'Death of a Party' (Albarn, Coxon, James, Rowntree)

In the summer of 1996, when the Blur fan club were looking for an exclusive release to feature on *Blurb #4,* Food records offered 'Death of a Party': an acoustic demo recorded at Matrix in June 1992. Feeling that the title was an apt description of how they now collectively viewed the Britpop scene, the group re-assessed the song, with Food's Andy Ross encouraging them to record it properly for their upcoming fifth album.

The sombre lyric has references to the AIDS paranoia that swept the world in the 1980s and 1990s, while 'Go to another party and hang myself gently on the shelf' is a clear nod to the sexual restraint that followed the crisis.

> The death of the teenager
> Standing on his own
> Why did he bother?
> Should have slept alone

The instrumentation is a moody, sombre affair touching on reggae and dub. There's plenty of drum distortion too, with Stephen Street detailing that he and engineer John Smith would overload mic pre-amps and various outboard units to get that crushed dirty sound. Graham is also in feedback and fuzz heaven, with his menacingly oversaturated guitar intro setting the morbid mood before flying off into trippy delay-pedal repetitions at 2:18.

Like on 'Theme From Retro', The Specials are a dominant influence, with their classic 1981 single 'Ghost Town' coming to mind. Damon's 'Lot 105' Hammond organ is a central arrangement feature – the lead phrase appearing to be two different parts merged together with a quick tremolo on one, creating an eerie, trilling effect that's perfect for the songs funeral-like ambience.

'Chinese Bombs' (Albarn, Coxon, James, Rowntree)

Debuted alongside 'Song 2' at the June-1996 Hultsfred Festival in Sweden, 'Chinese Bombs' was, in Graham's description, a gift from Damon, saying 'Here, let loose on this'. This short, sharp blast of hardcore noise was easily the dirtiest-sounding track the band had recorded up to this point – and with the possible exception of 'Bugman', it still is.

But this is no straightforward amateurish thrash. As Stephen Street attests, the track was tricky to pull off, featuring – in his estimation – 'incredible musicianship'. Graham backs this up by revealing that Damon wrote the song using a barre-chord sliding up and down the frets in a jerky, rhythmic pulse that was difficult to play, particularly for the fast tempo it was at. The intro and chorus drum pattern is also awkward, in that – instead of the kick – the snare drum comes in on the downbeat, with Street admitting that when he saw them play it live, he thought Dave might explode. Also, Alex's snarling midrange bass briefly takes centre stage over Graham's aggressive riffing in the pre-verse sections.

At Damon's own admission, the martial-art subject matter was written after watching many Bruce Lee films – Damon has since confirmed that the lyrics are pretty much taken from the dialogue. By the time the shouted chorus arrives, the track is so thrillingly distorted you can barely make out the words – suffice it to say, 'Bruce Lee comes to save the day ... the Chinese way!'.

'I'm Just a Killer for Your Love' (Albarn, Coxon, James, Rowntree)
Damon described this as 'Sly and the Family Stone meets Black Sabbath', though the song title seems to refer to the T. Rex classic 'Jeepster', which features the line 'Girl, I'm just a vampire for your love'.

This noisy, lo-fi jam is built upon a mid-paced drum loop (that strangely enters a split second late). The only other instrumentation comes in the form of waspish distorted guitar, wah-fuzz bass, and acoustic guitar low in the mix. There's also a strange, percussive fretboard swiping sound throughout.

Damon's amp-distorted vocal is in a dour, quasi-monotonic baritone in the verses, with a more-impassioned falsetto on each chorus: which is presumably the Sly and the Family Stone bit. The mysterious lyrics describe some sort of violent event; perhaps a murder:

Cut my hair off in the road
I take my coat off dropped my load
I wipe my hands on the grass
'Cause I know that nothing ever lasts

The song was recorded in just two and a half hours in November 1996 as a test for Damon's new 13 studio in West London, during B-Side sessions after *Blur* was deemed complete. It was added to the final tracklisting at the last minute.

'Look Inside America' (Albarn, Coxon, James, Rowntree)
The thawing in Damon's attitude towards the US came during a March 1996 European tour with The Rentals, when he befriended ex-Weezer bassist Matt Sharp – Damon claiming rather snobbishly that he saw Americans 'in a different way from that point onwards'. Inspired by this new state of mind, he wrote 'Look Inside America' – a mid-paced tour diary of a song, detailing his experiences on the road in the USA.

Starting with a verse that sounds like 'End of a Century' Mark II, the lyric portrays Damon weary and bruised, taking baths in hotel rooms, watching *Annie Hall* on the tour bus and playing 'second-rate chat shows', before surmising, 'Look inside America, she's alright'. The heartfelt and honest vocal struck a chord with Graham, who recalled listening to the finished track as being one of his fondest memories of making the album and claimed that Damon 'really summed up what touring in America was like'. Though Graham was clearly a fan, Alex didn't want the song on the record, explaining to *NME* in 1997: 'It was 'Fuck off, Britpop.' That's why it had to be included. 'Look Inside America' is exactly what Britpop was urging you *not* to do.'

Nevertheless, the song is an album highlight, featuring Damon's expertly crafted lyric, warmly-nostalgic melody, and a clever little key-change in the 'sitting out the distance' section. Such was the track's sophistication, Stephen Street acknowledged the need to break their new 'No unnecessary extra instrumentation' rule, employing a string section on the verses, and even more impressively, a harpist (sadly uncredited) during the day-dreamy breakdown sequence at 2:36. Graham then punctures through the floaty ambience with a nasty nasal guitar solo, highlighting the striking dichotomy between the two contrasting sections.

Stylistically unique on *Blur*, 'Look Inside America' was perhaps the final time Damon indulged the concise 'Ray Davies meets *Hunky Dory*-era' Bowie songwriting style that characterised so many of Blur's mid-career triumphs, stretching back to 'For Tomorrow'. As the penultimate *Blur* track bullishly declared, they were now 'Movin' On'.

'Strange News From Another Star' (Albarn, Coxon, James, Rowntree)

Taking its title from a collection of Herman Hesse short stories written between 1913 and 1918, 'Strange News From Another Star' was originally recorded as a keyboard-and-vocal-only demo. Feeling that the majority of it was good enough to keep, Stephen Street used big chunks of it in the finished article.

With its self-deprecating lyric, the track captures Damon in a melancholy and pensive state of mind:

I don't believe in me
All I've ever done is tame
Will you love me all the same
Will you love me though
Always the same

The 'death star' mentioned in verse one is a reference to the depression Damon suffered prior to arriving in Iceland, whilst the song itself is a general tribute to that country's serene majesty.

Fading in with a brief snippet of Icelandic radio, the recording starts in a scrappy fashion with some distorted keyboard chords, a creepy low-rumbling synth, false-start acoustic guitar noise, and even a sniff. It's not a million miles from the spooky ambience that opens 'Andy Warhol' from David Bowie's *Hunky Dory* LP. In fact, this is the most like early-1970's-Bowie that Blur had ever sounded. With its battered acoustic guitar arrangement and space-age alienation, the track has 'Space Oddity' written all over it. Not only is this apparent in the title (strange=oddity, star=space), but the sequence from 2:44 to 3:10 is almost a pastiche of the 'Space Oddity' fade-out. Alex's descending bass line is surely inspired by Herbie Flowers on that track, and the atonal, carefully random keyboard notes are also a giveaway, leading to a disorienting, swirling climax. Meanwhile, the phrase 'from another star' is a melodic quote from 'The Man Who Sold The World'.

But it's not quite over. At 3:10, it explodes into a tumultuous outro fade-out, featuring Dave and Graham reprising their 'Song 2' trick of playing simultaneous drum kits. Guitar, keyboards and bass drone on around them, bringing this mesmeric and evocative piece to a hypnotic close.

'Movin' On' (Albarn, Coxon, James, Rowntree)

Sandwiched between two of the album's most expansive musical pieces is 'Movin' On' – a straight-up rocker with some amp-distorted Mark E. Smith-esque vocals. The effect is akin to 'Jubilee'-meets-'Entertain Me' – this time, while Blur do their glam rock, they're channelling The Fall instead of Mott the Hoople. Despite the slightly surreal subject matter ('I met the gourmet man, with aluminium lungs'), the song is a swaggering statement of intent. The chorus, with its defiant proclamation 'This is the music, we're movin' on', provides confirmation Blur were shifting away from the shiny pop of yore, and encouraging fans to accept this loose, raucous new direction.

Fading in with Graham's open guitar roaring away, the click-count is audible, which is ironic considering how much the bpm gradually increases, particularly in the second chorus. Though the song is fairly simple, the performance is vibrant, and even goofy in places, like the three-note synth/guitar breaks and with the 'aaahhh' falsetto chorus backing vocals. Then there's Graham's wild theremin solo at 2:19, delivered with the same carefree abandon as the Jon Spencer Blues Explosion at their irreverent mid-1990s peak.

An overlooked gem in Blur's up-tempo rock box, 'Movin' On' was performed extensively when touring the album, but afterwards never graced the setlist again. More significantly, it was William Orbit's reworking of the track (opening the 1998 remix album *Bustin' + Dronin'*) that prompted the band to consider him for producer of their next album *13*.

'Essex Dogs' (Albarn, Coxon, James, Rowntree)

Alex reckons the album's hallucinatory finale to be one of the most accomplished pieces of music Blur ever committed to tape. The song began life as a poem that Damon performed with acoustic guitar and backing tape in The Poetry Olympics at the Royal Albert Hall on 7 July 1996.

The nightmarish subject matter harks back to Damon's endured experiences growing up in the garrison town of Colchester, while the line 'Here comes that panic attack' is likely a reference to a 'horrible panicky experience' he suffered walking past Stanway Comprehensive one night in 1994 after the success of *Parklife*.

In this town, we all go to terminal pubs
It helps us sweat out those angry bits of life
In this town, the English Army grind their teeth into glass
Now you'll get a kicking tonight

Knowing Damon wanted this weird track to be on the LP, Stephen Street admitted that the prospect of recording it seemed intimidating and he couldn't work out how to approach it. Then one afternoon after having lunch at Primrose Hill, the band returned to the studio and Street suggested giving it a crack. Interviewed in *3862 Days,* he recalled: 'We got the drum pattern together as a starting point, and then Graham pretty much immediately got that motorbike revving effect. They jammed for fifteen or twenty minutes, then I asked them to leave it with me, and I edited it together with the new hard disk recorder I had.'

This new piece of kit was the Otari RADAR – the same device Street used to record the 'Song 2' drum loop – enabling him to cut and paste chunks of the performance into any sequence he wanted.

This industrial-sounding epic begins with Graham's aforementioned 'motorbike revving' guitar intro – the piece centred around the repeatedly moving A-to-F# harmonic pattern. He created this distinctive effect with his trusty Boss DD-3 effect pedal, set to the hold function, so the note repeats *ad infinitum*. Then, using the delay-time knob, he was able to manually adjust the pitch.

Elsewhere, and in similar to fashion to 'Death of a Party', Dave's filtered, skippy drum pattern is mixed with wild reverb and delay on the snare, giving a certain dub flavour. Graham later revealed that the loose jam performance was inspired by him bringing the Tortoise album *Millions Now Living Will Never Die* into the sessions. A listen to their brooding and sonically adventurous track 'Djed' seems to confirm this claim. The icing on top of this dystopian cake is Damon's vocal – delivered in a hushed, almost comatose spoken baritone, with the addition of sinister, unsettling distorted vocals and quasi-nursery-rhyme backing vocal.

Followed at 6:25 by a floaty, droning instrumental, 'Essex Dogs' closed the album on a darkly experimental note – totally unprecedented in the band's discography thus far, and a million miles from the slick, glossy pop of *The Great Escape*. Even more significantly, this wilfully strange piece – with its chopped-up methodology and psychedelic atmosphere – offered a tantalising gateway into the world of *13*.

Contemporary Tracks

'All Your Life' (Albarn, Coxon, James, Rowntree)

B-side to 'Beetlebum'

According to Damon, this immaculately produced B-side was left off *Blur* because it sounded too much like their 1993-1995 Britpop incarnation. As autobiographically honest as anything from the album it was excluded from, 'All Your Life' appears to reflect the period that resulted in Oasis' 1995/1996 dominance of the UK music scene, following the release of their massively-popular singles 'Wonderwall' and 'Don't Look Back in Anger'. Seemingly overnight, Blur suddenly went from being number one and on top of the world, to being seen as the least cool band on the planet. It was a phase that almost destroyed them.

Damon's lyric reveals an ego battered and bruised by the subsequent media backlash and a man desperately looking for solace elsewhere:

Oh England my love, you made me look like a fool
I need someone to tell me everything will be alright
I need someone to hold me when the day turns to night
I need someone who loves me, more than you do

The latter line could be seen as a subconscious cry for help in his personal life – in particular, his now troubled relationship with Elastica vocalist Justine Frischmann, alluded to in the line 'You and me a '90s double bill'.

The song is a highly melodic slice of Bowie-inspired glam pop, opening with Dave's beautiful vintage 1970s drum rhythm. Then Graham's power chords crash in, followed by a stuttering chromatic riff that ascends in dramatic fashion. The song has a similar structure to 'Beetlebum', in that there's an instrumental pause at the end of the verses, allowing Damon's impassioned vocal to briefly take centre stage before the noisily-vibrant chorus.

The Bowie influence is most prevalent in the verses, especially on the line 'On the way to heaven in a company car', which is a direct melodic steal of 'Put another log on the fire for me' from *Hunky Dory*'s 'Oh! You Pretty Things'. If 'All Your Life' had appeared on the *Blur* album, it possibly would've attracted more unwanted attention from Bowie's lawyers, to accompany their 'M.O.R.' plagiarism claim.

Still, this doesn't detract from the fact that 'All Your Life' is undoubtedly one of Blur's best mid-period B-sides, and as strong a composition as anything on the *Blur* album.

'A Spell (For Money)' (Albarn, Coxon, James, Rowntree)

B-side to 'Beetlebum'

The most impenetrable of all the *Blur* B-sides is this Kraut-rocking ambient instrumental jam in C, which nevertheless has some interesting textures. The jarring, wobbly lead instrument appears to be a stylophone put through a distortion pedal, with an array of curious atonal synth effects sprayed liberally throughout its three and a half minutes. Dave's tabla-enhanced drum groove and Alex's meandering bass combine to create a rhythm section sounding like Can doing Bowie's 'V-2 Schneider'.

'Woodpigeon Song' (Albarn, Coxon, James, Rowntree)

B-side to 'Beetlebum'

The light and airy 'Woodpigeon Song' comes complete with cooing bird samples and a falsetto vocal melody which – despite the song's inherent cuteness – has a gently haunting flavour. It's a charming childlike piece recalling *Unicorn*-era Tyrannosaurus Rex. Though it's under two minutes in length, there is a longer version, including the full-band outro on the *21* box set.

'Dancehall' (Albarn, Coxon, James, Rowntree)

B-side to 'Beetlebum', and featured on US version of ***Blur***.

Possessing a spectral aura similar to 'Theme From Retro', 'Dancehall' is unique in the Blur canon in that it features a harmonica solo. Opening with woozy slide guitar leading into an ominous crescendo of noise, the song swings into life with Dave's '1-2-3-4!' count-in scream. The grungy G/E/A/Bb chord sequence is distinctly Nirvana-esque, and the rhythm section lurches along in a menacing lopsided gait. Damon's distorted vocal – sung in the same hazy drawl as 'I'm Just a Killer for Your Love' – describes an unsettling scenario akin to the ballroom scene in *The Shining* if crossed with *Resident Evil*:

> There are ghosts in here, an easy laze
> They dance all night with a vacant gaze
> They stand in rows and buy alcohol
> We're having fun at the dancehall

'Dancehall' is also one of the few Blur songs to sample another track: in this case, 'Suzy Creamcheese' by obscure San Francisco garage rockers Teddy and his Patches. Released in 1967, that song had appeared on numerous compilations, including *Acid Dreams* (1979), which is likely where it was swiped from. The sample – used in the breakdown section – gives the track a distant and unsettling vibe, heightened by the punctuating twitchy broken-cable noises.

'Get Out of Cities' (Albarn, Coxon, James, Rowntree)

B-side to 'Song 2'

This playful rocker was likely recorded in the hope that its quirky, upbeat charm had single potential. Its eventual B-side placing seems apt given that it shares a chorus chord sequence with the A-side, whilst the 'Move out to the trees' line bears a resemblance to 'Your head is there to move you around' from R.E.M.'s 'Stand'.

The four-on-the-floor verses and lyrics depicting the virtues of back-to-basics jungle-living ('I've been swinging in trees…running naked in the breeze') suggest a less-concise younger sibling of The Kinks' 1970 hit 'Apeman' cross-bred with Wire's 'I Am the Fly'. In the more raucous moments, and at the fuzzy, unhinged end of the scale, particularly in the quasi-industrial middle section and the scratchy slippery-riffed final chorus, Graham's guitar stars.

'Polished Stone' (Albarn, Coxon, James, Rowntree)

B-side to 'Song 2'

Following in the lugubrious footsteps of 'Bone Bag' and 'Resigned', 'Polished Stone' is a low-key minor marvel, self-produced at Damon's newly-constructed 13 studio in the same sessions that spawned 'I'm Just a Killer for Your Love'. Graham's slacker-rock slide guitar work dominates the arrangement, while Damon's lazily-mumbled double-tracked vocals sit atop. Like some of the *Modern Life Is Rubbish* B-sides, the lyrics lie in the hazy sphere of alcohol, while the 'It's numb' falsetto section draws parallels with the strung-out languor of 'Beetlebum'.

> Now I fall to the ground
> I can't get up, well never mind
> Today's gone and it won't be long
> Before we fall asleep and forget what we've done
>
> Now you bite my tongue
> And when the alcohol's gone
> I won't feel a thing

With its pretty 1960s melodies and decidedly unpolished performance, the softly soothing 'Polished Stone' is a worthy interpretation of a hangover's melancholic malaise.

'Bustin' and Dronin' (Albarn, Coxon, James, Rowntree)

B-side to 'Song 2'

Another November 1996 piece recorded at studio 13 after *Blur* sessions had wrapped, this cacophonous track could be heard as a stepping stone to *13*'s 'Battle'. The title 'Bustin' and Dronin'' is due to the chord sequence being rooted around one continuous droning E note.

Starting with a looped tabla sample, the track explodes into a sludgy psychedelic jam, with thrashing, scabrous fuzz-guitar and loud cymbal-heavy drums. Alex jams a sultry bass groove before Damon's vocal enters, buried low in the mix. The lyrics are as impenetrable as they are indecipherable, with lines like 'It's an awful week, marry me in Jeans', before the chorus cries a desperate falsetto 'Man alive!'. At 2:38, it settles into a hypnotic looping outro guitar refrain, calling to mind the ancient nursery rhyme 'Frere Jacques'.

A relatively-undiscovered and to-this-day unperformed B-side, 'Bustin' and Dronin'' is perhaps more significant for naming the 1998 remix compilation, which in turn led to the band choosing William Orbit as the producer for their next album, *13*.

'Swallows in the Heatwave' (Albarn, Coxon, James, Rowntree)

B-side to 'M.O.R.'

At the Electric Ballroom B-sides gig in September 1999, Damon and Graham revealed that this song was recorded 'in Barcelona, in a kitchen, on an industrial estate'. Further illumination came from Alex saying the track was cut at the same time as the demos for 'No Distance To Run' and 'Optigan 1' in June 1997 – with the band hungover and tired after a heavy night out partying in Barcelona. Originally intending to record B-sides for 'M.O.R', only this recording emerged, the single coming out as just one CD version instead of two.

A grungy lo-fi affair, the song takes vocal cues from Pavement, especially in the 'ooh woo ooh ooh' chorus, which is reminiscent of their 1993 single 'Cut Your Hair'. But the Pavement comparisons don't end there – the track resembles their 'Starlings of the Slipstream' from the *Brighten the Corners* album, not only in its title but in the crashing chords that hang in the air around the verse vocals. Still, it's an enjoyable melodic song, and Alex's bass should be singled out for special attention, taking centre stage with its sliding hooks and trebly distorted tone, and making it sound almost like a standard six-string guitar.

'Cowboy Song' (Albarn, Coxon, James, Rowntree)

Released August 1998 on the Dead Man on Campus soundtrack

A Dust Brothers-produced anomaly in Blur's catalogue, 'Cowboy Song' appeared on the above soundtrack, which also included exclusive tracks from Elastica and Supergrass.

A rather unfocused piece sonically, the track strangely features sounds and riffs that later appeared on the 'Tender' B-side 'All We Want'. Knowing that Stephen Street produced 'All We Want' – and thus was likely recorded around 1996 – it's possible the track was left unfinished, and needing new material for the movie, Food records sent the multitracks to the L.A.-based production duo to work on – with Damon singing new words over the top later. Whatever the truth is, 'Cowboy Song' is hardly vintage Blur, with Damon's muddled lyrics and monotonous vocal sounding uninspired, paling in comparison to its excellent descendant 'All We Want'.

13 (1999)

Personnel:
Damon Albarn: Vocals, Piano, Keyboards, Acoustic guitar, Melodica
Graham Coxon: Electric guitar, Backing vocals, Vocals on 'Coffee & TV', Co-lead vocals on 'Tender', Saxophone, Banjo
Alex James: Bass, Double Bass on 'Tender'
Dave Rowntree: Drums, Percussion
The London Community Gospel Choir: Vocals on 'Tender'
Jason Cox: Engineering, Additional drums on 'Battle'
Recorded June-October 1998 at Sarm West, Mayfair and 13 (London); Studio Syrland, Reykjavik
Producers: William Orbit, Blur
Release dates: UK: 15 March 1999, US: 23 March 1999
Label: Food/Parlophone (UK), Virgin (US)
Chart Placings: UK: 1, US: 80

On December 17 1997, Blur played the Brighton Centre: the last gig of an extremely busy touring year. After the show, Damon took Stephen Street to one side, respectfully informing him that it was time for a change and Blur would be looking for someone else to record their next album. As hurt as Street was, he wasn't the only one with misgivings about the decision. Graham – who was immensely proud of the *Blur* album and over the years had built a strong bond with the producer – was against the change, fearing a repeat of the Andy Partridge debacle.

Searching for fresh blood, Food Records' Andy Ross suggested William Orbit. The house and electronic music pioneer had just produced Madonna's hugely successful 1998 album *Ray of Light,* and his 'Movin' On' remix for *Bustin' + Dronin'* had pricked up the collective ears.

Preliminary sessions with Orbit begun in July 1998 at Damon's cramped 13 studio in West London. The band spent three weeks jamming and knocking songs into shape before decamping to the more upmarket Mayfair Studios in Primrose Hill. At this early stage, Orbit simply captured everything the band recorded on his computer, and the musicians wouldn't even review what they'd done. At other times, Orbit's attention would be somewhere else entirely, such as being busy listening to unrelated sounds on a sampler, with Graham, in particular, wondering what the hell was going on.

But that wasn't the sessions' only chaotic factor. Dave Rowntree has confessed that recording the album was a sad process, with him sensing that inter-band relationships were falling apart. Certain members (presumably Graham) would turn up abusive and drunk, and sometimes not at all. Meanwhile, Damon was preoccupied in the mornings, composing the *Ravenous* movie score with Michael Nyman – a dilution of Damon's energies that apparently irked the others, particularly as Alex and Graham had songs of their own going begging. Considering that Damon was also using heroin and suffering after the tumultuous split with Justine Frischmann, it now seems a minor miracle the album was completed at all. But completed it was. Somehow, amongst the turmoil – with the aid of Orbit's editing wizardry – the band delivered an emotionally raw, free-flowing and sonically dense record, quite unlike anything they'd recorded before.

With Damon's breakup as a thematic focal point, *13* (rejected titles included *Blue* and *When You're Walking Backwards to Hell, No-One Can See You Only God*) was released in March 1999 to a mixed review bag. Many praised the innovative electronic experimentation within its bloodied grooves; others found it self-indulgent and messy. Fans, on the whole, were satisfied, and bolstered by the success of singles 'Tender' and 'Coffee & TV', the album sold well, going platinum in the UK.

Strong sales notwithstanding, *13* marked the beginning of the end for the band as a foursome and full-time entity. Damon began work on the debut Gorillaz album soon afterwards, and Graham busied himself with a second solo LP, *The Golden D*, released the following summer. With the late-1999 Wembley singles-night gig and 2000's hits compilation *Blur: The Best Of* seemingly wrapping things up in a neat bow, it appeared the death of a party was lurking on the horizon.

'Tender' (Albarn, Coxon, James, Rowntree)

A-side single. Released 22 February 1999. UK: 2

Clocking in at a whopping 7:42, 'Tender' is Blur's longest single, and to this day, one of their most enduring songs. A heartwarming celebration of lost love, it was completed early in the *13* sessions and stems from a turbulent time for Damon personally, when in early-1998 he left the house he shared with girlfriend Justine Frischmann. Their seven-year relationship was over. However, the emotional debris yielded one of Blur's most uplifting pieces – a spiritual pop epic in the same anthemic mould as The Beatles' 'Hey Jude' or John Lennon's 'Give Peace a Chance'.

The first sound heard is a fragile guitar phrase that producer William Orbit claims was taken straight from Graham's demo tape for his 1998 debut solo album *The Sky Is Too High*. Graham contradicts this somewhat, speculating that it was William's Panasonic dictaphone on the track, due to it having a 'better wobble'. Either way, it's a wonderfully-wonky lo-fi opening for such a huge, sweeping pop song, and it provided Graham with the all-important melody for the plaintive 'Oh my baby' post-chorus vocal refrain (which sounds not unlike the country and western standard 'Oh My Darling, Clementine'). Graham has revealed the melody was sitting in his head one morning after waking, an occurrence likened to 'little elves' entering his head.

Developed from Damon's home demo and recorded at London's Mayfair Studios, the backing track fell into place by accident. The entire rhythm section consists of Graham and Dave banging around on the studio floor with big planks of wood. Accompanying this pounding, boom-crunch backbeat is Alex's double bass: an instrument he usually kept in his kitchen. However, rather than play the part live, William Orbit simply recorded Alex tuning his double bass, sampled the various notes and programmed a bass line from that. Also of note are the banjo and rhythm guitar tracks – a standard acoustic and an American tin guitar played by Damon, giving the arrangement a feel almost of the Mississippi Delta.

With the basic track more or less complete, they took the tapes to Reykjavik, where Damon worked on his vocals. His performance is richly smooth and one of his most luscious. It certainly made an impression on Alex, who claimed it had a profound healing effect upon him when he first heard it in Reykjavik's Studio Syrland.

The title and opening line 'Tender is the night' refer to the 1934 F.Scott Fitzgerald novel, which itself was titled as a quotation from the fourth verse of John Keats' 'Ode to a Nightingale'. In keeping with those works' timeless qualities, Damon's transcendental lyric navigates to the simple message that 'Love's the greatest thing that we have', while he wills himself and others who are feeling such emotional distress, to 'Come on... get through it'. Back in London – and with the vocals in the can – it was felt that the arrangement needed a special extra something to take it into the stratosphere, but the band were left scratching their heads. Orbit told *Select* in 1999: 'We were wondering about doing strings at first, but in the end, because of the nature of the song, we thought 'Why not try it with a choir?'.'

Because, in Orbit's words,'The song was such a goer', Food Records agreed to finance the vocal group of Damon's choice: The London Community Gospel Choir. Founded in 1982, the now world-famous 30-piece choir has backed performers as huge as Justin Timberlake, Madonna and Elton John. In reference to the choir's brilliant vocal arrangement, Orbit recalled that he and the band would chip in with suggestions, and the choir would be 'very gracious' in taking them.

When the track was complete, everyone involved was convinced the song would be a big hit, with Alex proclaiming it 'An obvious global fucking number-1'. The British music press and fans alike were similarly expectant, with the song gaining widespread radio airplay. But unfortunately, a third Blur UK number 1 was not destined to be. Released there as the album's first single, 'Tender' was held from the top spot by Britney Spears' debut '...Baby One More Time'. Despite this, 'Tender' was a major seller, shifting over 400,000 units and gaining gold status in the UK.

But much more significant than any chart position or sales is how pertinent the song became at various points in Blur's later history. With Graham no longer part of the band in the *Think Tank* era, Damon would request that the crowd sing Graham's parts when performing the song, making his absence even more glaring. Then, at Blur's triumphant 2009 Glastonbury headline reunion show, the crowd loudly sang the same 'Oh my baby' section back at the band unprompted after the song had finished, highlighting the immense sense of unity and power it possesses. Remarkably, Damon and Graham also performed it alongside long-time nemesis Noel Gallagher (with childhood-hero Paul Weller on drums) at the 2013 Teenage Cancer Trust charity event, proving that Damon's cries of 'Heal me' in the song's closing section really did repair old wounds.

'Bugman' (Albarn, Coxon, James, Rowntree)

The sadistic sonic terrorism that is 'Bugman' is a jarring contrast after the lighter-waving gospel anthemics of the radio-friendly 'Tender'. Existing in two halves, the first portion (where the actual song resides) is a meaty wedge of fierce glam-punk noise with Dave's decidedly big-beat-inspired verse drumming.

Blasting into view with a fiendishly fuzzy guitar riff, the track is a showcase for one of Graham's most thrilling and aggressive performances ever on a Blur record. As William Orbit told *Uncut* in 2009:

> We got tracks like 'Bugman' because we harnessed Graham's rage: sometimes by subterfuge. Graham would play the wrong notes every time we were recording. Then, as if to say 'Just to let everybody know I can do it', every time the tape was rewinding, he'd do it perfectly, so I kept the machine rolling. 'Bugman' showed Graham could get people in the whole room to pay attention, like Jimi Hendrix. They are the grittiest guitars.

Damon's lyric seems to revisit the druggy wordplay of 'Beetlebum', with references to the 'nodding dogs', while the Bugman himself could very well be his dealer. There's a key-change up a 3rd for the 'Go hang around go 'round' choruses (sung in a Bowie-esque 'Suffragette City' half-sung, half-yelled style) before the song eventually dives into a cacophonous, chaotic outro featuring what can only be described as a vacuum-cleaner solo.

At the three-minute mark, the arrangement descends into a vast slab of distorted, broken audio-cable white noise, fooling you into thinking the song is over but bounces back into life at 3:24 for the second half. Lead by Alex's groovy bass line (his favourite part of the record); this section is a kaleidoscopic, Pro Tools construction which Damon describes as 'pure jamming'. The closing 'Space is the place' refrain is the title of a 1972 Sun Ra movie, and is a melodic nod to Madonna's then-recently William Orbit produced hit single 'Ray of Light'.

'Bugman' was to be the album's second single, before the poppier 'Coffee & TV' usurped it at the last minute. Each band member had already completed remixes of 'Bugman' intended as B-sides, which were used for the eventual 'Coffee & TV' single. Damon provided the proto-Gorillaz Latin-flavoured 'X-Offender'; Alex the swaggering dance-pop of 'Trade Stylee'; Graham and Dave offering darker textures on 'Metal Slip Hop' and 'Coyote' respectively.

'Coffee & TV' (Albarn, Coxon, James, Rowntree)

A-side single. Released 28 June 1999. UK: 11

Of all the *13* tracks, 'Coffee & TV' is the most like *old* Blur – a tightly-constructed, upbeat melodic chugger that could easily be mistaken for a pristine Stephen Street production.

Perhaps the biggest misconception about the song is that Graham wrote it, which is only partly true. While he was responsible for the lyric, Damon wrote the chords and melody. Graham explained that the reason he penned the words was because Damon simply had too many lyrics still to write for other songs on the album, telling Graham, '*You* write the lyrics!'. Written in one evening and recorded in just two takes, Graham's dry verse vocal was delivered in a gentle baritone, with verse one detailing a hard life in the city:

Do you feel like a chain store?
Practically floored
One of many zeros
Kicked around bored
Your ears are full but you're empty
Holding out your heart
To people who never really
Care how you are

Verse two describes an equally damaging escape out to the sticks:

Do you go to the country
It isn't very far
There's people there who will hurt you
Because of who you are

Then there are Damon's delightful West Coast three-part harmony choruses (think Beach Boys meets Crosby, Stills & Nash), which exult the benefits of drinking coffee and watching TV as an antidote to a lack of social confidence. In many interviews, Graham has described this mundane combo as a coping method that helped control his alcoholism.

While the arrangement itself is fairly straightforward indie rock, Damon's chords are rather inventive, and the way Graham voices these chords is unusual – particularly the A minor where he plays an implied A major in the two lower chord notes, simultaneously playing a C (the minor 3rd) on the third string. An interesting clash!

The other big arrangement feature is the feral, distorted guitar solo, which is at complete odds with the tight rhythm section. Graham explained to *NME* in 2012: 'I just put something there because we wanted to fill a gap, and said,

'We'll come back to it', and the song developed, so we kept it. I wasn't even looking at the guitar, I was just stomping on pedals'.

Along with 'Tender', 'Coffee & TV' is easily *13*'s poppiest moment, so it was no surprise it was chosen over 'Bugman' as the album's second single. With the aid of its excellent music video (starring Milky the Milk Carton), the single reached 11 in the UK, though Blur's manager Chris Morrison claims it should've gone top 10, as it was confirmed that some sales weren't recorded. Today it's one of Blur's best-known songs and is – at the time of this writing – their third most-streamed Spotify track. Also featured in the video – but not on the single – was a short Damon solo-organ piece often referred to as the 'Coffee & TV Exiltude'. Appearing on the album after the song fades out, this brief snippet was the first of a number of short musical fragments on the LP.

'Swamp Song' (Albarn, Coxon, James, Rowntree)

Like 'Movin' On' from the previous record, this strung-out glam stomp is one of the most overlooked rockers in Blur's discography and was originally slated as a B-side before being promoted for inclusion on *13*.

Swishing up on a wave of vocal feedback and noise delay, Graham's abrasive slide guitar lick begins the track – sounding like a slower, sludgier precursor to the riff on The Hives' 2001 hit 'Main Offender'. Damon's swaggering, sexy vocal grows more raggedly passionate – akin to a crazed Elvis – as the song progresses. The melody is deceptively close to that of 'Song 2', but here the vowels are elongated and stretched out like a comedy elastic band.

As was his wont in the *13* period, Damon seems to reference heroin use in the lyric ('Stick it in my veins!', 'Give me fever'), whilst the 'I wanna be with you' backing vocal could be a comment on his feelings towards ex-girlfriend Justine Frischmann. The 'Wakka Wakka' line either obliquely name-checks the indigenous people of Australia, or is the Swahili saying that means 'burn brightly'.

Elsewhere, the arrangement bops along like a slinkier, daintier version of 'Go Out' from *The Magic Whip,* though sonically it's stuffed full of strange, demented vocals, distorted textures and musical phrases – most notably the eastern-flavoured three-note falsetto backing vocals at 1:40, which suggest a desert rather than a swamp.

'1992' (Albarn, Coxon, James, Rowntree)

Named after the year when it was originally demoed – and not, as some reports claim, the year Damon met Justine (that was 1990) – '1992' was resurrected after Damon found a lost tape of the song. Reflecting the despair and turmoil Blur had endured in that period, this is *13*'s first instance of true anguish: a majestic, mournful companion piece to 'Sing' from *Leisure*.

Built on slow, pounding drums and languid walking bass, the song is structured around an endless piano and acoustic guitar chord sequence, with Damon's sombre baritone floating over the top. The lyric is mysterious and hazy, alluding to the emotional weariness of Blur's annus horribilis, and the emotional bitterness that could've stemmed from his recent split with Justine:

What do you owe me?
The price of your peace of mind
You'd love my bed, you took it all instead

There are a plethora of fascinating arrangement touches, such as Damon's fervently fragile, amp-distorted melodica solo, and the 'Oily Water'-via-My-Bloody-Valentine guitar noise at around 2:15, which Graham affectionately dubbed 'the UFO landing'.

Though the band rarely performed the song live, Graham has claimed it's his favourite track on *13*, and one of his favourite Damon compositions. Speaking to *Q* magazine in 2018, he said, 'I adore that song. It's very melancholic, but it's also vindictive and dark. It's very complicated emotionally, and the chord sequence reflects that.'

'B.L.U.R.E.M.I.' (Albarn, Coxon, James, Rowntree)

Closing the first half of *13* is this punky new wave romp, which provides a little light relief in the midst of such intense emotion. Taking a cue from the Sex Pistols' similarly-themed 'EMI', 'B.L.U.R.E.M.I' is a prank-ish reference to the relationship between band and label – Damon describing the piece as 'a musical gag'. Indeed, it's difficult to tell whether he's being sincere or disingenuous.

Whatever side of that line the lyrics fall on, they seem self-referential, with lines like 'Group using a loop of another pop group' being a possible nod to the Stone Roses-via-Run-DMC sample on Blur's early hit 'There's No Other Way', while the line 'Cause I'm of regular features and Adidas trainers' harks back to the 1992 single 'Popscene' and its proclamation that 'Everyone is a clever clone'.

Opening with a brief snatch of Damon's stereo-delayed vocal scatting (which may well have been taken from the 'Battle' vocal session), the track starts proper with Graham's spiky opening guitar riff using a similar chord voicing to those of 'Bugman' and 'Coffee & TV'. It's a raucous and ragged group performance, boasting an impressive, nimble bass line under Damon's peppy melodica solo, while Graham's delay-pedal wizardry combines with Dave's limber drum fills; to stunning effect from 1:37 to 1:47.

As expertly performed overall as it is, it's the vocals that catapult 'B.L.U.R.E.M.I' out of the ordinary and into the unusual. Firstly, the verse lyrics are delivered in a distorted monotone, with Damon's lower vocal sounding particularly gruff and menacing. Even more bizarre is the vocoder lead on the 'Beeelluuarreeeemeye!' choruses, which predates a similar part on *Think Tank*'s 'Crazy Beat'. Vari-sped up an octave from a low belch to a high squawk, it gives the impression that Donald Duck has flown in for a guest appearance, enhancing the song's impish humour.

'Battle' (Albarn, Coxon, James, Rowntree)

One of the most experimental pieces to ever feature on a Blur album, 'Battle' could lay claim to being Blur's very own 'Tomorrow Never Knows'. A dizzying psychedelic sonic experiment, it picks up where hazy mid-tempo 1996 recordings 'I'm Just a Killer for Your Love' and 'Bustin' and Dronin'' left off, this time sending listeners into outer space.

Written in Bali on Damon and Justine's final holiday together at the beginning of 1998, the chorus hook describes the antagonistic nature of their crumbling romance, though the notion is equally relevant to inter-band relationships at the time. All Blur members were battling inner demons and addictions – notably Graham with alcohol and Damon secretly struggling to quit heroin. The two school friends were also in a musical tussle, as producer William Orbit told *Uncut* in 2009: 'There was a battle between Damon's more experimental direction and Graham's punk one. If that tension had been growing on previous LPs, it came to a head here.'

This tension manifested itself in a piece of music with many conflicting moods and a daring abstract soundscape. Opening on a one-note synth arpeggio, the intro combines Damon's ominous high synth line with an indecipherable mumbled vocal and a brief early snatch of guitar echo, creating a foreboding, ghostly ambience. Then the rhythm track kicks in. Dave's drumming is simple yet aggressive and powerful, with some intriguing gating techniques used on the heavy cymbals towards the end. Alex's dubby verse bass line is submerged enough in lower frequencies to make the notes more or less nebulous and indistinguishable. Graham's guitars roam all over the place, ranging from perverse, distorted thrashing (2:19) and queasy echo-drenched disorientation (5:35) to disturbed wailing (6:00). Explaining some of these parts, Graham has since admitted that he often found himself in an intensely bad mood on the *13* sessions, and has cited 'Battle' as one of the most obvious examples.

But it's not all dark doom. Not only do the choruses contain Damon's sweet falsetto nursery-rhyme melody, but blissful synth sweeps recall the soft-synth textures buried beneath All Saints' William Orbit-produced 2000 hit 'Pure Shores', the similarity an example of the producer's inimitable sonic stamp.

In keeping with the music's amorphous quality, the lyric's are cryptic, though the final falsetto line ('See it overcome...') does seem to offer a glimpse of hope:

> Caucasian slouch
> Gear and love about
> See it all come down to it
> Adore myself...

With the aid of a brief outro-like instrumental at 6:34 (from the 'Caramel' sessions?), 'Battle' pips 'Tender' to the post at being the album's longest track

– clocking in at 7:44 – and is the one most responsible for the Radiohead comparisons prevalent at the release of *13*.

'Mellow Song' (Albarn, Coxon, James, Rowntree)

Described by Alex as 'beautiful', 'Mellow Song' developed from the earlier piece 'Mellow Jam' that appeared as a 'Tender' B-side. Offering a brief moment of restraint on an otherwise intense record, the first half consists only of Damon on acoustic guitar and vocal, with some backing vocals and synths in verse 2.

The lyric offers sombre glimpses of the malaise that plagued Damon after his breakup with Justine. It was a lonely period of pain and reflection, soothed only by making music and periodic bouts of hedonism resulting in the inevitable morning-after hangover:

> Shooting stars in my left arm
> It's an alcohol low
> Giving away time to Casio

Despite the overriding anguish, he gives a relaxed, almost subdued vocal performance, with a melody faintly echoing Nirvana's 'On a Plain'. Though the delicate mood continues when the full band enters halfway through, the sonic palette radically widens to include reverse fuzz guitars, ornate harpsichord, an eastern-flavoured melodica solo and snatches of laughter. The dark compressed drum sound is particularly evocative, consisting only of muted toms and cymbals – Dave has since stated it's his favourite of his own playing on *13*.

'Trailerpark' (Albarn, Coxon, James, Rowntree)

The hip-hop-flavoured 'Trailerpark' was commissioned for *Chef Aid*: the 1998 soundtrack album for the TV Series *South Park*. But after that record's executive producer Rick Rubin rejected the song, the band decided to include it on *13*. Self-produced with engineer Jason Cox before the William Orbit sessions began, it's arguably the album's most disappointing moment.

The intro is promising, with a lo-fi, boom-bap looped drum sample, doom-laden organ and a vaguely jazz-like keyboard phrase. Then it settles into a ploddy, double hi-hat hip-hop rhythm with a country-flavoured A-minor guitar lick buried low in the mix. Damon's hazy baritone vocal is curiously indistinct, as is Alex's muddy bass tone.

The key lyric line is the wry humour of 'I lost my girl to The Rolling Stones'. Damon was apparently inspired to write the lyric after watching a Rolling Stones documentary. However, it's actually a metaphor referring to the drugged and debauched rock 'n' roll lifestyle that got in the way of his relationship with Justine Frischmann.

Undoubtedly, the main factor behind this overwhelming whiff of anticlimax was Blur's far-superior 1998 Glastonbury performance of the song. Having a gloriously twangy guitar sound, heavier drums, a confident vocal and further developed lyrics ('As the rain falls down the valley…to the great unwashed'), this version makes you wonder what might've been had they re-recorded it with William Orbit. His sonic ingenuity, mixed with the band's greater familiarity with the material, could've made 'Trailerpark' a contender for a single – perhaps coming off as a cross between 'Coffee & TV' and 'Trimm Trabb'. The live version's more sprightly tempo would also have given the album's second half some much-needed energy, especially in the speedy final section, which was ripe for a full-on psychedelic gonzo-punk wig-out.

'Caramel' (Albarn, Coxon, James, Rowntree)

This magisterial studio construction (not performed live until a 2012 BBC gig) is surely one of the most sorrow-soaked pieces Blur ever recorded. More overtly so than 'Beetlebum', the title is a metaphor for heroin's sticky goo-like consistency when heated and smoked.

Having muddied the after-affects of his opioid use with the yearning despair of a broken relationship, 'Caramel' finds Damon nakedly detailing the simultaneous need to move on from Justine and quit the demon drug, while accepting that he perhaps never will.

I've gotta get over
I've got to get better
Will love you forever
I've gotta find genius
I've gotta get better
I've gotta stop smoking

The line 'I've gotta find genius' is interesting in the wake of his subsequent comment to *Q* magazine about the drug: 'Heroin freed me up... it was incredibly creative.'

Despite the track's unpredictable structure and evocative instrumentation, the song itself is extremely simple, centred around a gloomy church-organ chord sequence. Acknowledgement must be given to William Orbit for his electronics manipulation (especially at 3:43) – a nuanced dynamic journey and a sonic world that seamlessly melds the disparate performance elements.

The arrangement creeps up ominously, appearing on the horizon like slow debris from a mushroom cloud of muffled loops. A haunting acoustic guitar riff punctures the air at 0:20, sliding up and down like wailing beasts yelping in pain. Damon delivers this section's baritone vocal in the most fragile of groans, revisiting the hushed numbness of 'Sing'.

As the music intensifies and the rhythm section enters in earnest, Dave's jazz-like brush drums become a focal point, flowing fluently on a river of snare rolls and tom hits, propelling the piece into its climactic middle section where Damon scats a slowly-rising falsetto phrase ('Day come') like a delirious schoolboy in a psychedelic church choir. Despite his public dislike of post-Syd Barrett Pink Floyd, it's possibly the closest Blur have ever come to sounding like them (*Meddle* era), and parallels can also be drawn with Graham's prog-rock heroes Van Der Graaf Generator.

After 'Caramel' fades away, the listener is treated to two bonus spoonfuls of music. The first – at 6:30 – is a wistful wartime organ waltz, floating in the air like a shorter alternative to 'Optigan I'; the second is a funky metallic jam that thrusts forth with the sound of an engine revving up, making it perfect fodder for a late-1990s car commercial.

'Trimm Trabb' (Albarn, Coxon, James, Rowntree)

Taking its title from the popular 1970s Adidas sneaker, 'Trimm Trabb' (the extra b in 'Trabb' presumably added for copyright reasons) repeats the 'Blue Jeans' device of equating air-cushioned shoes with melancholy.

Though perhaps too lyrically dour to ever be considered for a single, it was nevertheless built on a naggingly-addictive acoustic guitar riff (inspired by the Syd Barrett track 'Wined and Dined'), accompanied by a spooky echoed monophonic piano line straight out of Mulder and Scully's worst nightmares. Dave's skippy filtered drums give the arrangement a trip-hop gait, and Damon's spooky opening 'oooh' vocals suggest he'd spent time meditating with Yoko Ono. Even stranger is his pitch-shifted spoken '1033 North West Drive', suggesting – like 'Trouble in the Message Centre' – that he'd taken to quoting excerpts from his US-tour hotel room receipts.

Once the song starts proper, we're back in pity party territory, as Damon forlornly intones 'I got no style' – a self-effacing start to a lyric that seems to lament the emptiness of consumer culture, and his participation in it. Once again, his relationship woes are referenced, whilst drug use is also insinuated ('I doze, doze away').

But, at 2:53, instead of feeling sorry for him, Graham stomps on his distortion pedal and proceeds to flare up emotions so that by the time the fiery metal-tinged coda arrives, Damon is raging all of his bile out in a primal scream that would surely make the aforementioned Yoko's late husband John Lennon proud. It could be argued that this is the point where Damon finally cracks, breaking down for the show-stopping finale that follows.

'No Distance Left To Run' (Albarn, Coxon, James, Rowntree)

A-side single. Released 15 November 1999. UK:14

The mother of all of the album's emotional bloodletting finally manifests itself. According to Alex, this was originally demoed on tour in Barcelona during the same session that produced the B-side 'Swallows in the Heatwave'. It indicates that in June 1997, Damon already knew his relationship was doomed, or the song originally had different lyrics. Either way, this desperately sad blues lullaby was deemed too good to play second fiddle to 'M.O.R.' and was wisely held back for *13*.

When the time came to record the song proper, Damon had been through the breakup and was out the other side, but the pain was still raw – William Orbit claiming that Damon was in floods of tears during the session. Listening to the close-mic'd vocal, you can clearly hear his voice quiver on the lines 'I don't wanna see you / 'Cause I know the dreams that you keep', with the performance, in general, being the most moving and honest of his career.

The lyric confirms all that some of the album's other songs implied. 'When you're coming down, think of me here' acknowledges the role drugs had in their breakup, while 'one who settles down, stays around / Spends more time with you' is an admission of Damon's lack of loyalty and commitment, which possibly proved to be the final straw.

The rhythm section takes an elegant back seat throughout, but Graham's stirring guitar part is full of soulful string bends and delicate high-fret chord work. Played on his vintage Gibson ES-335 (the same instrument used on 'This Is a Low'), it's a part he's immensely proud of, telling *The Observer* in 1999: 'It's a beautiful noise and it's support for Damon – I'm doubling up his sentiments. You can say a lot more in songs than you can actually tell someone about. It's a good way of communicating with your friends.'

When the final album running order was drawn up, all involved were aware of the song's power and universality. Released as the album's third single, 'No Distance Left To Run' couldn't quite crack the UK top 10. Perhaps this was a blessing in disguise, as it spared Damon the expectation of having to play it at every subsequent Blur concert, having publicly stated how upset the song made him, and the finality it represented.

Over twenty years later, Damon has definitely moved on, and singing it today must feel unnatural with the specific subject matter digging up seriously old bones. Nevertheless, the title was used to name the band's 2010 feature-length documentary, indicating the significant place the song held in Blur's fervent history.

'Optigan I' (Albarn, Coxon, James, Rowntree)

Appearing like the sunrise over a misty, battle-strewn horizon, this was another track Alex claims was demoed on tour in Barcelona in June 1997. He felt it was a shame they didn't develop it into a more substantial piece.

Featuring loops of a gently-tolling bell, piano, woodblock and drums, the track is a scratchy, shuffling instrumental waltz that Damon apparently performed alone on an Optigan optical organ. Manufactured in 1971, the Optigan was an electronic keyboard instrument that played looped samples on circular floppy 12" plastic film discs that could be inserted underneath its buttons and keys.

Despite being only a fleeting snippet of music, 'Optigan I' was presumably chosen as a full track over the album's other brief interludes due to its fully-developed melody. Closing *13* on a wonderfully wistful note, this relaxing retro piece provides much-needed solace after the intensity that had gone before.

Contemporary Tracks

'French Song' (Albarn, Coxon, James, Rowntree)

B-side to 'Tender'

Presumably, this William-Orbit-produced instrumental was titled due to its resemblance to the 1960s Yé-yé movement – a tongue-in-cheek high camp brand of Gallic pop that included such luminaries as Sylvie Vartan, France Gall and Françoise Hardy. Experimental Anglo-French art-pop band Stereolab were also influenced by the genre.

Strutting along like a distant relative of The Outsiders' 1967 hit 'Bend Me Shape Me', the track is built on a retro-sounding Motown drum loop and contains a number of short repetitive musical passages over its eight minutes. Graham's chirpy, choppy guitar riffs dominate the mix, Damon provides kooky fairground-organ interludes, and Dave adds cowbell. Alex was surely loving this one.

Gradually speeding up into a chaotic crash (*a la* 'Intermission'), 'French Song' was never in the running for inclusion on *13* due to its fruity frivolity. Still, it would've made a perfect addition to the soundtrack of *Eurotrash* – a late-night 1990s UK TV review show hosted by Anton de Caunes and Jean-Paul Gautier, full of oddball comedy and wacky world topics.

'All We Want' (Albarn, Coxon, James, Rowntree)

B-side to 'Tender'

One of the greatest mysteries surrounding this sterling Stephen Street-produced rocker is why it wasn't released sooner. Likely recorded in the 1996 *Blur* sessions (the last time they would work with Street until 2014), it was left in the vaults pending its inclusion on the 'Tender' CD single three years later. One possible explanation is that – like the earlier B-side 'Magpie' – the backing track was complete, but Damon didn't get around to recording a vocal until much later. The fact that parts of this recording were subsequently used in the inferior earlier-released 'Cowboy Song', suggests this could be the case.

There's also the possibility the track was recorded in sessions for *The Great Escape* and then simply forgotten about. Graham's scabrous, scratchy fuzz guitar tone is similar to that of 'Stereotypes', and Damon's 'Villa Rosie'-esque verse vocal comes via a youthful-sounding Britpop delivery, though the band feels looser than on much of the music they made at the time, and the lack of *Great-Escape*-era engineers Tom Girling and Julia Gardner on the credits would seem to refute this theory.

Whatever the facts, 'All We Want' is one of Blur's best later-period B-sides, featuring a pleading chorus lyric and passionate melodic vocal sitting atop a bed of sweet Beatlesque harmonies, and a yearning guitar arpeggio from Graham.

All we want, all anybody wants
Is to feel something, but I just say nothing

The verses are dark and dystopian ('Give me gas if it gets too much'), with the opening synth hook mimicking the desperate wail of an ambulance siren. The atmospheric sax-sprayed middle section adds a touch of drama, while Damon's gentle keyboard glissandos wind down to the epic finale.

'Mellow Jam' (Albarn, Coxon, James, Rowntree)

B-side to 'Tender'

Recorded at Damon's 13 studio during preliminary sessions for *13*, 'Mellow Jam' is just that: a chilled-out band improvisation, built around the chord of A. Produced by William Orbit, with Dave on brushes and Damon on a soft Fender Rhodes-type sound, this recording is notable for being the starting point of 'Mellow Song'.

Though much of Damon's vocal is essentially indecipherable scat, the 'You'll see' line was developed into the 'We'll see' phrases that occur in the final *13* version. Graham's two-note guitar slides were also imported, as was the chord sequence that appears suddenly at 3:22.

'So You' (Albarn, Coxon, James, Rowntree)

B-side to 'No Distance Left To Run'

Self-produced with trusty long-term engineer John Smith, the recording of 'So You' was filmed for the Blur *South Bank Show* TV special broadcast in the UK at the end of 1999. It's a fascinating glimpse into the creative process and inter-band dynamic, showing the track's formation from start to finish. We see an enthusiastic Damon teaching the chords to an intense-looking Graham while a more relaxed Alex joins in on the side. It then cuts to the band jamming the song with Graham showing his assertion – instructing Dave to 'Keep it going really solidly'. Finally, the band nail the arrangement, with Damon recording his vocal, nonchalantly proclaiming, 'Okay, it's done'.

'So You' is a serene slow-jam centred around a groove dominated by two guitar parts – one a distorted octave-pedal runabout, the other a vibrato-infused gentle hula strum. The lyric appears to echo its A-side's sentiments of a relationship breakdown ('Keeping it all inside / So you') and drug use ('Coming off it gently'), while there's a speculative coded reference to Gorillaz and Damon's future in Blur ('Getting out the side door'). The closing voices seem to be Damon talking to the documentary crew, a nice piece of symbolism reflecting the unique recording session.

'Beagle 2' (Albarn, Coxon, James, Rowntree)

B-side to 'No Distance Left To Run'

Both keen amateur astronomers (as 'Far Out' demonstrates), Alex and Dave joined the Beagle 2 team in 1998 after visiting the Houston NASA Space Center while on their 1997 US tour. Noticing the amount of British space scientists who had to travel to the States for work, they returned home to seek out a UK space program to get behind. They found Dr Colin Pillinger, a planetary scientist who'd been working on the Beagle: a 27kg landing device designed to look for signs of life on and under the surface of Mars. To help publicise the project and gain financial support, Blur agreed to compose a unique piece of music to be utilised as a call sign back to Earth when the Beagle 2 landed on its target planet.

Again filmed by the *South Bank Show* TV crew, footage shows Damon sitting at the piano composing a mystery tune before we see a heavily-smoking Blur grinding out the 'Beagle 2' recording in the studio. Sitting atop this sludgy interstellar jam is Damon's nine-note melody (played on a suitably spacey Korg synthesizer), loosely based on a Fibonacci sequence, a series where each number is the sum of the previous two (1,2,3,5,8,13,21 etc.). The pattern is seen time and again in nature, on sunflower petals, seashell spirals and pine-cone shapes.

Transported by the European Space Agency's June 2003 Mars Express mission, the Beagle 2 craft went missing on Christmas day 2003 after successfully deploying from the mother ship. After its location was unknown for more than eleven years – and just months after Dr. Pillinger's death – it was reported in January 2015 that the lander was located intact on the Mars surface. Rightfully proud of his involvement in this historic event, Dave told *The Yorkshire Post* in 2019: 'It got to Mars, the parachutes worked, it landed on the ground safely. No other country got to Mars on their first attempt, apart from us.'

'I Got Law' (Albarn, Coxon, James, Rowntree)

Bonus track on Japanese edition of 13

'I Got Law' is a solo-Damon four-track cassette demo that was later developed into the debut Gorillaz song 'Tomorrow Comes Day' released in 2000. Featuring just a drum machine, retro synth and scratch vocal, strangely, it was a bonus track on the Japanese edition of *13*. This indicates that Food Records were really short on spare material, a surprising circumstance considering the amount the band recorded in the album sessions.

'Music Is My Radar' (Albarn, Coxon, James, Rowntree)

A-side single. Released 16 October 2000. UK: 10

Needing a new single to tie in with the release of the greatest hits collection *Blur: The Best Of*, the band had already recorded 'Black Book' when they went in to record its proposed B-side with rookie producer Ben Hillier. Hillier was introduced to the band via his work with Alex on the 'Bugman' remix 'Trade Stylee', and had recently engineered Graham's second solo LP *The Golden D*.

Recorded in summer 2000, 'Music Is My Radar' is a swaggering *Remain in Light*-era Talking Heads-style groove, demoed under the working title 'Squeezebox'. With Damon in the thick of recording the debut Gorillaz album, he would've been subconsciously – if not fully – aware that Blur were no longer a full-time concern for him. This might explain the somewhat unfocused lyric, which seems to espouse the benefits of dancing and letting the music guide him, delivered mostly in a lazy, semi-nonsensical scat. Still, the mention of legendary Nigerian drummer Tony Allen is significant due to his subsequent work with Damon in supergroup The Good, the Bad & the Queen, and the 'Aah don't stop me now' hook stays in your head for hours.

Around the release of *Think Tank*, the music press were quick to point at this track as a clear indicator that Graham was on his way out. On the contrary, his inventive playing spices up the sparse arrangement to stirring levels, whilst drawing a visceral energy from his bandmates' performances. From the fuzz-bomb riffing at 3:09 to the clipped three-note arpeggios at 2:06, he's on fire throughout. Best of all is the guitar and bass duet at 1:11, bringing to fruition The Meters' influence teased on 'There's No Other Way'. Dave's skittering drum fills are impressive too, especially at the climax of the Mick Jagger-aping 'Emotional Rescue'-esque falsetto section.

Thankfully promoted over 'Black Book' to A-side status, 'Music Is My Radar' was released in support of *Blur: The Best Of*. Perhaps too thematically flippant to appeal to the cerebral end of Blur's fan base, it only reached number ten in the UK, the worst commercial performance of new Blur material since 'For Tomorrow' in 1993.

By no means a classic Blur single, 'Music Is My Radar' was still a pivotal release, hinting at the afrobeat-inspired direction they would take on *Think Tank*, and offering a tantalising glimpse into how that album might've sounded if Graham had remained for the sessions' duration.

'Black Book' (Albarn, Coxon, James, Rowntree)

B-side of 'Music Is My Radar'

Produced and mixed by producer Chris Potter (The Verve and Richard Ashcroft) over the summer of 2000, the brooding 'Black Book' was demoed under the working title 'Jawbone'. Slated as a single to promote the greatest hits collection *Blur: The Best Of*, it was eventually demoted to B-side status.

Almost two years after the heartbreak of *13*, the song finds Damon revitalised and in love again after meeting artist Suzi Winstanley in late 1998. The title is a reference to a theoretical contact list of past lovers, the lyric confirming that he would 'Throw it on the fire' because his new woman was his 'one desire'. Despite the evident joy and contentment these words portray, 'Black Book' is kind of an inverse 'Tender', and would've struggled to match that track's universal appeal if released as a single. Damon's vocal is delivered in deep, hushed tones at the very bottom of his register, while the London Community Gospel Choir makes another appearance, throwing some moody minor-chord harmonies into the mix. The band arrangement is dark and serious, featuring a sombre-sounding Wurlitzer electric piano and Graham's woebegone western guitar licks.

The ambience brightens slightly, slowly building for the extended 'Give me my soul' coda. Meanwhile, Graham lets loose some raucous blues riffs until the piece fades, allowing the choir to return with Damon for one last refrain.

Due to its absence on any official Blur album, 'Black Book' is a rather overlooked soulful slow burn of a song and one that Spiritualized frontman Jason Pierce would've been proud to call his own.

Think Tank (2003)

Personnel:
Damon Albarn: Vocals, Piano, Keyboards, Guitar, Melodica
Alex James: Bass, Backing vocals
Dave Rowntree: Drums, Percussion, Backing vocals, Guitar on 'On the Way to the Club'
Graham Coxon: Guitars on 'Battery In Your Leg'
Phil Daniels: Vocal on 'Me White Noise'
Mike Smith: Saxophone
James Dring: Drum programming
Group Regional du Marrakech: Oud, Violin, Rabab, Tere, Darbouka, Kanoun
Recorded: November 2001-November 2002 at 13 (London); Blur's makeshift barn studios at Marrakesh and Devon
Producers: Ben Hillier, Norman Cook, William Orbit, Blur
Release dates: UK: 5 May 2003, US: 6 May 2003
Label: Parlophone (UK), Virgin (US)
Chart Placings: UK: 1, US: 56

Directly before beginning sessions for a proposed seventh album, inter-band relationships were at an all-time low. Fresh from the massive worldwide success of Gorillaz, and feeling that 2000's *Blur: The Best Of* was perhaps a full stop rather than a comma, Damon has since admitted that he wasn't particularly interested in making another Blur record. Reluctantly, he put himself back in the saddle, as a brotherly show of solidarity towards his estranged bandmates. Alex – who was possibly feeling jealous and hurt in equal measure by Damon's extra-marital affair – had made unflattering noises about Gorillaz in the UK press, adding to the sour atmosphere.

But worse was to come. Assembling with producer Ben Hillier at studio 13 in November 2001, Damon, Alex and Dave patched up their differences, only to discover that Graham was nowhere to be seen. Having struggled with alcohol addiction for the majority of his adult life, Graham was admitted into The Priory for a second time but had failed to notify anyone involved with Blur of his whereabouts. To be fair, he did return to the studio for sessions in February and May 2002, but sadly, the damage had been done. Angered and defiant, the other three had already made significant progress on new material in his absence, and bar 'Battery in Your Leg', Graham's contributions were deemed ill-fitting. Eventually, manager Chris Morrison notified Graham that his services were – until further notice – not required. Graham took this as a sign that he should leave Blur once and for all.

As a result of all this turmoil, the remaining members decided they needed to escape London and work elsewhere. In August, with Ben Hillier in tow, they flew to Marrakesh, Morocco, spending several months recording in a makeshift barn studio, and were later joined by Norman Cook: aka Fatboy Slim. It was now that the record's thematic nature took shape – rustic, sun-baked and exotically groovy, this was a new worldbeat Blur.

Returning to the UK in late 2002, recording was completed in another barn, this time on Damon's Devon farm. By now, the music press were aware of Graham's departure, heightening interest and speculation as to the record's content.

Released in May 2003, *Think Tank* was met with glowing reviews, praising the new direction while downplaying Graham's notable absence. Dave and Alex were both quoted at the time as saying it was the best material they'd ever produced. However, fans were not so sure, with the record polarising opinion amongst many who missed the erstwhile guitarist's unmistakable sonic imprint. Despite topping the charts, *Think Tank* was Blur's first record since *Modern Life Is Rubbish* to fail to go platinum in their homeland and yielded no major hit singles. Sensing the band was now a spent force, Damon thereafter returned his attentions to Gorillaz, while Dave and Alex perused other professional endeavours. Alas, there would be no more activity in camp Blur until Graham's dramatic return for 2009's triumphant reunion shows.

'Ambulance' (Albarn, James, Rowntree)

The musical germ of 'Ambulance' came to Damon while working on the debut Gorillaz album – held back for not fitting inside that record's playful pop puzzle. Picking up where 'Black Book' left off, it's a slow-burning mood piece that pensively basks in the fiery light of love.

It opens with a lopsided, sticky hi-hatted 1980s drum-machine pattern that Dave doubles on the live kit, soon joined by Alex's dubby bass and African percussion. Futuristically rigid and urban in groove, this was new territory for Blur.

After almost a minute, Damon's airy falsetto verse vocal arrives, tenderly proclaiming, 'I ain't got nothing to be scared of / 'Cause I love you', before switching to a Bowie-esque baritone during the 'I was born out of love' bridge section. Though the lyric obviously celebrates Damon's now four-year relationship with artist Suzi Winstanley, there are hints of frustration, not to mention the admission of his own shortcomings:

> I know I'm not there
> But I'm getting, getting, getting there
> If you let me live my life
> I'll stay with you to the end

The instrumentation is a heady mix – Mike Smith's honking baritone sax, gospel-tinged backing vocals, squelchy Stevie Wonder-style synth lines, waspish and jabbing guitar thrashing etc. For this reason, Graham's absence is not felt as strongly as on other *Think Tank* tracks and, despite the rather simple three-chord harmonic structure, it's a solid start to the record.

The song – like many on the album – had a long gestation period, but the band have all stated they knew it would be the opening track. Speaking in a 2003

XFM radio interview, Alex said, ''Ambulance' was the first song that I thought, 'Right, this is Blur again ... I'm in the right place again'. I suppose the lyrics have something to do with that, you know, having nothing to be scared of anymore.'

After all the anguish and upset of Graham's departure, 'Ambulance' might've been to the band what its title suggests: a rescue vehicle to take them to hospital (Morocco) and relieve them of their ills.

'Out of Time' (Albarn, James, Rowntree)

A-side single. Released 14 April 2003. UK: 5

Blur's big comeback single after a three-year hiatus – and their first official release without Graham's involvement – is arguably *Think Tank*'s finest moment. A typically melancholy Damon composition, it was recorded in two distinct stages – the one-take-wonder backing track was cut in London at studio 13 and was later taken to Marrakesh for overdubs, vocals and mixing.

Beginning with a bizarre 'arrgghh!' sample taken from TV show *Doctor Who*, the track settles into its haunting mid-tempo groove early on, with Damon's rustic acoustic guitar sitting atop a light bossa nova rhythm section coloured by Dave's ringing brush snare and Alex's full-bodied bass.

Though Damon has stated that the words were written from a domestic perspective, his lilting lead vocal delivers a lyric that could potentially be viewed from two angles. On one hand, the chorus could be seen as a comment on Graham's departure – his well-publicised personal issues with alcohol addiction and need for domestic stability that eventually trumped his commitment to Blur. Then there's the rather more universal notion that it's a dread-filled rumination on war, over-consumption and a fear that the world could end at any moment:

> And you've been so busy lately
> That you haven't had the time
> To open up your mind
> And watch the world spinning gently out of time

The below lines seem to be a pertinent comment on the state that so many of us spend our days in now – not living in the present, but capturing everything on smartphones, to be stored on a cloud, likely to never be viewed again.

> Feel the sunshine on your face
> It's in a computer now
> Gone to the future, way out in space

In much the same vein as 'Tender', it was decided that the piece needed additional galvanising in the form of a non-contemporary musical source. In a 2012 *Q* magazine interview, producer Ben Hiller remembered:

We wanted to get some local players involved, so we got an Andalucian orchestra to come in and play on 'Out of Time'. We set them up in the courtyard, and they improvised the whole thing on ouds and zithers and violins. Afterwards, I realised I hadn't even sent the mix to the headphones, so they were essentially playing along to nothing.

Sharing the limelight with Damon's middle-eastern acoustic guitar solo, the Groupe Regional du Marrakech's performance provides a wonderfully ethereal element, further enhanced by the band's evocative and authentic Arabic-styled distorted backing vocals.

Released as the first *Think Tank* single, the song was the perfect embodiment of the album's core manifesto. All expected it to be a big hit, with Damon telling author Daniel Rachel in his 2013 book *Isle of Noises,* 'I thought 'Out of Time' would be an absolute killer, but it wasn't'.

Despite the track's obvious bucolic beauty, it isn't generally well-known outside of Blur's core fan base, perhaps being too solemn in theme to appeal to the masses. Nevertheless, it's one of the few Think Tank songs that Blur have performed regularly since reforming in 2009 – all the more poignant given its possible reference to Graham and his regretful lack of involvement in its creation.

'Crazy Beat' (Albarn, James, Rowntree)

A-side single. Released 7 July 2003. UK: 18, US mod rock: 22

This raucous Norman Cook-produced single was written and recorded entirely in Morocco, and is one of the album's few tracks that would've suited Graham's involvement (ironic due to his apparent unease about working with Mr Fatboy Slim).

Notwithstanding the track's 'B.L.U.R.E.M.I' aping, Donald Duck squawking vocoder hook, 'Crazy Beat' is a straight-up rocker with a decidedly *un*crazy drum pattern. Talking to *MTV* in 2003, Damon said, 'It started off in such a different way. The nearest thing I could compare it to is a really bad version of Daft Punk. So, we got sick of it, and then put in that descending guitar line over it to rough it up a bit.'

Besides urging Damon to change the main lyrical hook (originally 'Forget the rock, we don't wanna stop'), Cook's obvious contribution seems to be the broken-record repeat on 'Crazy', and a sliced-up strobe-like effect on the screamed vocal at 2:01. On electric guitar duties, Damon provides the 'I Wanna Be Your Dog' Stooges-like central four-chord guitar riff. Lyrically, the chorus vivaciously vows to 'get the people dancing on their feet', while the verses offer amusing wordplay:

I'm on my mobile
I'm talking to the president

I'm gonna get him for the money I spent
Trying to get him to party with me
I even offered him ecstasy

Forcefully constructed to be an in-your-face, lads-on-the-dance-floor banger, the single failed to make much of an impact in the UK; fans were perhaps smelling the faint whiff of desperation in its garish grooves. But it fared much better in the US, where it was the album's lead single. Blur's first since 'Song 2' to make the Modern Rock Tracks chart, we can attribute 'Crazy Beat''s success to having a similar punky vigour.

'Good Song' (Albarn, James, Rowntree)

A-side single. Released 6 October 2003. UK: 22

The appropriately-titled 'Good Song' began life as a demo named after the hip hop group that Damon would work with on the future Gorillaz singles 'Feel Good Inc' and 'Superfast Jellyfish'. Speaking to *XFM* in 2003, he said, 'Well, that was originally called 'De La Soul', you know, right until the end. And I just always thought it was a good song and just called it 'Good Song'. I love the sort of intimacy of it, and I just think everyone really played gently on it.'

A sun-kissed, blissed-out kind of tune, Dave's languid hip hop drum rhythm meshes perfectly with Damon's addictive acoustic guitar loop: sampled from his demo. The combination creates a memorable, rustic opening, before Alex comes in with a bass hook that consists unusually of two simultaneous sliding notes.

Damon's mellifluous vocal is croaky and cracked with emotion – seemingly sung from the perspective of a pacifist soldier occupying his post in an invaded nation while falling in love with an inhabitant:

Waiting, got no town to hide in
The country's got a hold of my soul
TV's dead and there ain't no war in my head now
And you seem very beautiful to me

The coda line 'picture in my pocket looks like you' refers to his partner back home, while the lush Brian Wilson-summoning harmonies of 'You seem very beautiful' reportedly include Dave and Alex somewhere in the mix.

An obvious album highlight, 'Good Song' was the album's third and final UK single. Skulking in the chart at 22, its intimate charm was perhaps too laid-back to grip the record-buying public, who at the time were in thrall to the pomposity of The Darkness' 'I Believe in a Thing Called Love' and the crass moral grandstanding of The Black Eyed Peas' 'Where Is the Love?'. Still, 'Good Song' is a minor-marvel – to file alongside other melancholy Blur classics like 'Blue Jeans' and 'Badhead'.

'On the Way to the Club' (Albarn, Dring, James, Rowntree)

Sounding like a precursor to *Demon Days*-era Gorillaz, the moody electronica began life as a drum machine piece created by Damon's younger cousin James Dring. Featuring Dave's tentative guitar part (his first and last six-string appearance on a Blur record), the track took shape after Damon 'started mucking around with it in the studio after being out too late one night'.

Opening with Dring's jerky vintage drum machine rhythm, Alex's propulsive three-note bass riff drives the track in its formative stages. Damon's melancholic vocal describes a solo venture out to a hedonistic nightspot, where he indulges in the short-lived pleasures of alcohol or drugs:

On my way to the club
I fell down a hole
All the people there said you come alone

So I stayed in the club
Just rewarding myself
Happiness could turn into something else

Elsewhere there's buzzy, distorted and filtered guitar, and the anxious, major-to-minor harpsichord-ish keyboard pattern in the breakdown successfully replicates the horrors of substance withdrawal. Then in the coda with the haunting 'ah' vocals, the stuttering, stumbling drum programming brings the track to its ominous close.

Damon Described this as a 'hangover song', claiming on the *Think Tank* interview CD that it was also 'an apology to my wonderful partner. It's like, what's the most pathetic excuse you could think of... 'Sorry, I fell down a hole!'.'

'Brothers and Sisters' (Albarn, James, Rowntree)

Thanks to Alex's hip-shaking bass line, this is a seductive and groovy track. Despite being one of the first things recorded for the album, it was a late addition to it.

Originally a much dirtier track – that Damon described as sounding like The Velvet Underground – the final version is a chilled Happy Mondays-meets-Grandmaster Flash rap, fused with the ancient Delta Blues stylings of Robert Johnson and Son House, most apparent in Damon's creaky guitar riff and the deep jazz-like close vocal harmonies at 0:25. A list of sorts, the lyric details how everyone needs a certain drug to get them through life – ranging from the commonplace (caffeine, sugar), to the treacherous (cocaine, codeine, crack). It's an intriguing idea that Damon claims was inspired by the life of John F. Kennedy and his need to have '28 drugs every day of his Presidency just to keep him functioning'.

With its anthemic, universal chorus and simple vocal melody, the track could've been a solid choice as a single.

However, as Weezer discovered with their similarly-themed 2005 single 'We Are All on Drugs', D-word censorship ('We're all dug-takers') might've made airplay elusive.

'Caravan' (Albarn, James, Rowntree)
'Caravan' is a dusty, dusky, lo-fi wonder, portraying the album's sunbaked Moroccan canvas to perfection. Though the title alludes to a group of travelling merchants, the lyric seems to reflect Damon's feelings towards Blur as a commodity, describing the all-encompassing power the band now held over him ('When it comes, you'll feel the weight of it'), with 'I got family / The caravan comes back for me' possibly alluding to the reliant people in his orbit: band members, road crew and management. Meanwhile, the line 'I try to quit, but my heart won't buy it' could be an admission of Damon's unfulfilled desire to leave Blur behind in the wake of Gorillaz' huge success, while perhaps acknowledging Graham's courage in doing exactly that ('I thought I was strong, but you are the one').

Though the arrangement is sparse and rugged, the production is deceptively modern, with a bitcrusher effect distorting the vocal, while muted clave, clicks and clap percussion nod towards the minimalist drum sounds of Damon's 2014 solo LP *Everyday Robots*. Alex's sultry bass part adds to the languid, half-lit atmosphere, as does the guitar work, which Damon has said was inspired by prominent Malian blues guitarist Afel Bocoum. Meanwhile, the two-part melodica solo captures the sound of the sun going down to seductive, soporific effect. Speaking to *XFM* in 2003, Alex said, 'That was like a perfect studio moment. Sitting on top of a strange barn in the Moroccan desert, listening to Damon do a vocal, and it was a perfectly still time of day, and the sun was perfectly red. There was just an immense sense of calm, and this music.'

'We've Got a File on You' (Albarn, James, Rowntree)
A short, sharp palette-cleanser after a run of restrained tracks, this took – in Alex's words – 'two minutes to write and a minute and a half to record'. Due to Graham's absence, the recording imbues more of the spirit of Gorillaz' 'Punk' than say 'B.L.U.R.E.M.I' or 'Chinese Bombs'. The only lyric is the title; the band yobbishly yelling it repeatedly, while a shrieking blast of what sounds like a zurna wind instrument punctuates the arabesque breakdown section. Despite the lightweight and generic central riff, 'We've Got a File on You' is a welcome blast of throwaway fun that the band performed live on the UK chat show *Friday Night With Jonathan Ross* in 2003.

'Moroccan Peoples Revolutionary Bowls Club' (Albarn, James, Rowntree)
This bizarrely titled *Combat Rock*-era Clash soundalike began life with the band's first arrival in Morocco in summer 2002. Initiated by Dave, who began drumming on flight cases as they were being wheeled off the transport trucks, producer Ben Hillier described the track to *Sound on Sound* in 2003: 'It turned

into a test-the-gear tune, and as soon as we got the desk up and running, we recorded some proper drums, and it all went off from there.'

Consequently and appropriately, Dave's drumming is to the fore – groovy and loose, yet technically sophisticated, and one of the album's few instances where he's not beholden to playing alongside a drum machine. Alex is his usual funky self, all offbeat licks and cheeky pauses, while Damon's afrobeat-inspired guitar lines are playfully buoyant, as is the vocoder.

Notwithstanding the music's vibrancy and Damon's bovver-boy vocal, he described the apocalyptic lyric as being about extinction, singing 'If we go and blow it up / Then we will disappear.' An outspoken pacifist and public opposer of the 2003 Iraq War, these lyrics are – alongside 'Out of Time' – some of Damon's most overtly anti-war ever on a Blur record.

'Sweet Song' (Albarn, James, Rowntree)

Along with 'Good Song', 'Sweet Song' is an album highlight. A William Orbit co-production, it was one of the last pieces recorded for *Think Tank*, completed at the makeshift barn studio on Damon's Devon farm in late 2002. Describing the song's genesis on the *Think Tank* interview CD, Damon said: 'I started writing it in the studio, waiting for everyone to turn up, and there was a *Dazed and Confused* magazine front cover on the wall with Graham on it. It was definitely inspired by Graham and missing him.'

Indeed, this delicately-touching piece (described by Alex as 'fluffy') was – according to Ben Hiller – recorded at a 'horrible' time, when legal negotiations for the split with Graham were starting. Damon would've been emotional recording this vocal, and it's a moving performance – not in the desperate way 'No Distance Left Run' is, but forlornly muted and cracked.

As personal as anything on *13*, the revealing lyric sees Damon admit he's a 'darkened soul, my streets are pop music and gold', tenderly proclaiming to Graham, 'I didn't mean to hurt you / It takes time to see what you've done.' However, there is a possible sting in the tail – the final line 'I just believed in you' could be seen as a passive-aggressive statement, indicating that Damon perhaps felt let down by Graham's disinterest in Blur. In the 2010 film documentary *No Distance Left To Run*, Damon confirms this notion: 'I hadn't particularly wanted to make another Blur album, because I had Gorillaz ... but I made a commitment and I thought I'd be terribly letting everyone down, so I got back into the saddle. And then he (Graham) just didn't turn up.'

Within the track's elegantly fragile arrangement, Dave and Alex admirably take a back seat; the instrumentation instead dominated by Damon's gentle, vintage-toned, Erik Satie-esque piano lines, accompanied by Williams Orbit's pulsing keyboards and spectral sound effects.

'Jets' (Albarn, James, Rowntree, Smith)

Think Tank's longest piece (6:23), the lumbering 'Jets' was recorded at three in the morning when the band were 'all pretty wired'. Containing just one vocal phrase repeated *ad infinitum* – 'Jets are like comets at sunset' – the line came to Damon when he noticed that planes flying overhead appeared 'like burning balls'. Mike Smith's bebop-inspired cod-jazz saxophone coda was recorded in one take after Damon instructed him to play like Charlie Parker.

With the first half being – according to Alex – the most simplistic thing the band had ever attempted – the track might've benefitted from some lyrical development, perhaps even a guest vocalist/rapper to add some excitement, while Dave's plodding drum rhythm is in dire need of some variation. Still, Damon's lo-fi acoustic guitar loop is catchy and Alex supplying a strident, sliding bass riff that – alongside the plethora of synth textures and sound effects – just about keeps the listener's attention.

'Gene by Gene' (Albarn, James, Rowntree)

A curate's egg of a tune, this – along with Norman Cook's other co-production 'Crazy Beat' – was written and recorded entirely in Morocco. The rhythm track is built upon unusual samples that were made back at studio 13, as Ben Hiller explained to *Sound on Sound* in 2003: 'I told Dave that if you hit a cymbal and lower it into a bucket of water, it pitch-shifts. So we got an old fish tank and filled it up with water, and spent all day hitting cymbals and lowering them into the water, sampling them and making loops.'

Out in Marrakesh, Cook added samples of Damon jumping up and down on a 'really squeaky old truck' that was parked behind the farmhouse they were recording in. Beyond the strangeness of this percussion, the song itself is a conventional pop piece, with an attractive doo-wop-meets-afro-pop chorus, hamstrung by some questionable lyrics:

> Every night and day
> I never dug it, in the USA
> I delete myself

Nevertheless, the daffy, pinballing 'buh buh buh' post-chorus section is enjoyably catchy, and Norman Cook himself is mentioned in verse two, set to a melody recalling The Clash's 'Bankrobber'. With some sharper wordplay and a more developed and less rigid drum pattern, 'Gene by Gene' could've been contender as a single.

'Battery in Your Leg' (Albarn, Coxon, James, Rowntree)

Notable for being the album's only recording to bear Graham's unmistakable presence, this mournful ballad was recorded at studio 13 early in the album's development. Speaking to *Uncut* in 2009, Ben Hiller explained the rather fraught situation:

> Graham hadn't left the band at that point. He came up from rehab for a couple of days, and we did 'Battery in Your Leg'. I think he was elated with that song,

> because it felt like it meant he could carry on in the band. But he very quickly became destructive. It was a relief when he decided to leave, and very sad. It had a very big impact on Damon especially because Graham was like a member of his family.

Tellingly, the track is one of the album's most organic cuts – a live studio performance where Dave's roomy drum part is allowed space to breathe, free from the shackles of loops or a drum machine. Alex and Graham reprise their 'Music Is My Radar' bass-and-guitar duet – except this time, instead of playing in unison, Graham opens the conversation with heavily-reverberated vibrato runs, which Alex duly answers in moving fashion. Graham's part is loud in the mix – a dramatic element – particularly when his slide guitar phrases combine with Dave's verse drum fills to explosive effect (at 0:45 and 1:18).

Damon's heartbreaking vocal performance and sombre piano chords heighten the emotion, topped off with a sentimental lyric that raises a glass to the 'good times and all the dignity we had', whilst tearfully proclaiming 'You can be with me, if you want to be'. Obviously directed at Graham, this could be Blur's answer to 'Shine On You Crazy Diamond', the song Pink Floyd famously wrote for their AWOL hero Syd Barrett. Damon touchingly described the one-take recording session as 'upsetting' – a poignant moment where the guys attempted to repair their fading relationship.

Though Graham being involved in the bulk of the album was not meant to be, placing 'Battery in Your Leg' as the album's final track was as good an indicator as any that the shadow of the irreplaceable guitarist loomed heavy over the rest of the band, even in the happy, blazing Moroccan sunshine.

'Me White Noise' (Albarn, Daniels, James, Rowntree)

Placed as a secret track before 'Ambulance' on the original *Think Tank* CD, the melody-free disco-terrorism of 'Me White Noise' features a return to the fold for actor and 'Parklife'-narrator Phil Daniels. It's a tense, dark, yet strangely amusing piece that may well have been influenced by the hot new artist on the British music scene during the early 2000s: Mike Skinner, aka The Streets.

The stomping two-chord backing track has an array of instrumentation – melodica, four-on-the-floor drums, fuzz bass, spiky-clean guitar power chords and creepy synths – and is coherently arranged. But the vocal track is a brilliantly deranged drunken shambles. Recorded in Devon late one night when Damon and Daniels were royally drunk, the latter slurs out familiar cockney-geezer rants and disconnected rambling raps like 'You look at the wall, what does the wall say to you? I ain't a mirror, fuck off!', Damon bringing a modicum of order to the chant-like 'Then you move move move' choruses.

An alternative version minus Daniels surfaced as the B-side to 'Good Song'. Though it's the same instrumental arrangement, Damon's hazy vocal is half-sung and has different lyrics. Here's the pick of the bunch:

Being English isn't about hate
It's about disgust
We're all disgusting

If they'd tried one more vocal session with some sharper lyrics and a more tuneful melody, they might've had an indie-club banger on their hands and a potential single. Instead, it's a fascinating but flawed addition to the album, and one of the few Blur songs ever to feature an expletive.

Contemporary Tracks

'Don't Bomb When You're the Bomb' (Albarn, James, Rowntree)

Single released 13 November 2002

This Kraftwerk-like electronic curio is built around a single chord, with the title being the sole lyric line. More interesting is the story surrounding its limited release. Pressed ahead of the album's completion in a run of 1000 white-label 7" singles, one of the boxes of vinyl had 'Bomb' written on it and UK customs picked it up. They passed it on to the police, who promptly carried out a controlled detonation. Now that's what I call (bangin') music!

'Money Makes Me Crazy' (Marrakech Mix) (Albarn, James, Rowntree)

B-side to 'Out of Time'

Begun in London but completed with Norman Cook in Morocco, this is arguably Blur's last truly great B-side. According to Ben Hiller, it didn't make it onto the album because 'it was just too happy, it was too bright and bouncy, but it's a great tune'.

Built on a peppy three-chord guitar riff reminiscent of Cornershop's 1997 hit 'Brimful of Asha', the track is an upbeat sunshine strum-along, akin to 'Coffee & TV' on a Caribbean vacation. Damon's breezy improvisational vocal adds to the lighthearted ambience, while the line 'I wanna be left on my own, on a holiday' recalls Weezer's 2001 megahit 'Island in the Sun'. The arrangement is vibrant and detailed, full of quirky electronic bleeps, carefree backing vocals, and a distorted guitar lick at 1:10 that may well be Alex on fuzz-bass. Elsewhere the piano and synth breakdown adds a certain dreamy drama, briefly bursting the bop-along bubble.

If this had been recorded earlier in Blur's career, they probably would've been forced to include it on an album, and perhaps they should've done so here. It certainly sounds like a single, and possibly would've fared better than the somewhat stiff 'Crazy Beat'.

'Tune 2' (Albarn, James, Rowntree)
B-side to 'Out of Time'

Complete with an eyebrow-raising title, 'Tune 2' is a wordless Arabian-tinged track containing chromatic auto-wah/phased guitar licks and a dub-like bottom-heavy bass tone. The middle-eastern-sounding lick at 1:01 appears to be a bouzouki, and Damon's only singing is the 'la la la' vocal and some indecipherable mumbling at 2:09. Unfocused in structure, the key changes up one step at 2:01, settling on a one-chord acoustic strum nestled on a bed of bells and bongos.

'The Outsider' (Albarn, Coxon, James, Rowntree)
B-Side to 'Crazy Beat'

Propelled by Dave's tom-heavy and vaguely surf-like drum pattern, this track's tense atmosphere would make ideal music for a desert-war flick or an Arabian car-chase movie. Featuring Graham on chugging rhythm guitar in the snappy 'day day day today' choruses, the nonsensical verses that Damon sings idly through a walkie-talkie impair the song:

> I got something on my ego
> The plastic surgery will melt
> It's like getting kinda me so
> It comes over when you come

Huh? More interesting are the darkly-eq'd piano parts that crop up throughout – pitch-shifted to sound like the notes are bending and melting in the Middle Eastern sun.

'Don't Be' (Albarn, James, Rowntree)
B-side to 'Crazy Beat'

Evident in Damon's distorted rap during the rustic funk opening, it seems that 'Don't Be' was the song recorded under the working title 'Chicken and Fries', and not, as some reports claim, 'Some Glad Morning'. Harmonically unadventurous, it's built on a droning pump-organ chord pair of A minor to G, and the lyric is similarly indistinct ('Don't be so dull'). The honking saxophone gives the louder, rockier sections a touch of sonic excitement, as does the skronky guitar riff at 1:37, which sounds fed through a distorted microamp. An acoustic version was released – alongside a demo of 'Sweet Song' – with the *Observer* newspaper in September 2003.

'Morricone' (Albarn, Coxon, James, Rowntree)
B-side to 'Good Song'

This is named after the Italian film composer, though the Middle Eastern flavour is at odds with his famous orchestral western style. With a verse vocal melody cribbed from Blondie's 1981 hit 'Rapture', and vague lyrics about 'blowing up the sky', the track is a languid, low-key affair, centred around C# minor. Enriched with eastern strings and distorted 'aaah' backing vocals reminiscent of 'Out of Time', the song also boasts the catchy 'You don't have it' chorus and a rhythm track that (at 1:15) sounds like someone stepping in a puddle. It's another of the *Think Tank* outtakes to include Graham on guitar, his fumbling, exploratory lead part here sounding like a first take.

'Some Glad Morning' (Albarn, Coxon, James, Rowntree)

Released December 2005 as fan club single CD#8

This quirky pop song is possibly the pick of the *Think Tank* B-sides that feature Graham. He told *The Guardian* in 2009: 'I'd had a couple of awkward afternoons recording, but I got a few things down. I was probably a little crackers, still. And very energetic.'

There are stylistic nods to the *Leisure* days in the baggy freak-out segment at 1:22, including bluesy guitar chords, funky fuzz-bass and a 'High Cool'-style sampled drum fill at 1:30. The section from 2:26 to 2:52 possesses the innocent, playful air of a late-1980s/early-1990s hip-hop-infused children's TV theme.

Damon's hazy, drawled vocal lets the side down slightly, while the inane lyrics are typical for a Blur B-side of the period: 'If you're in a Zoo, what can you do?'. Nevertheless, 'Some Glad Morning' is an interesting slab of whimsy that maybe should've been snuck onto *Think Tank* instead of 'Jets'.

'Colours' (Albarn, James, Rowntree)

Released 28 Aug 2003 as fan club single CD#7

Another fan-club-only single, 'Colours', is a demo that was never recorded properly and wasn't included in the *21* box set. A pretty, gentle and melodic tune evoking the twee folk stylings of early David Bowie tracks like 'Conversation Piece' and 'Letter to Hermione', the song was resurrected when Electric Wave Bureau covered it in the British 2012 movie *Broken*.

Hiatus and Reunions (2004-2013)

Blur played their final gig of the *Think Tank* tour at the Bournemouth International Centre on 12 December 2003, thereafter entering a four-year period of inactivity (though there were some aborted studio sessions in 2004 and 2005) which saw the remaining three members pursue vastly differing professional endeavours.

Naturally, Damon kept the highest-profile, releasing a second Gorillaz album: 2005's mammoth-selling *Demon Days*. Other notable projects included a 2007 LP with rock/folk/afrobeat supergroup The Good, the Bad & the Queen, and the 2008 soundtrack to the Chinese opera *Monkey: Journey to the West*.

Alex developed a multimedia persona, including cheesemaking, various TV appearances and writing newspaper columns among his activities, and in 2007, came his autobiography: the brilliantly titled *Bit of a Blur*. Dave also kept himself busy, in 2006 studying to become a criminal lawyer and unsuccessfully running as a Labour MP in 2007 and 2008.

Meanwhile, Graham stuck to his indie-rock guns. After a handful of cult-ish lo-fi solo albums in the early 2000s, he unleashed his major label debut *Happiness in Magazines,* in 2004. Featuring the punky 'Freakin' Out' and the Blur-esque pop of 'Bittersweet Bundle of Misery', the record went gold in the UK. It happily reunited him with Stephen Street, who also produced the follow-up: 2006's *Love Travels at Illegal Speeds*.

Now that everyone was seemingly busy and content in their own lives and careers, the sensational December 2008 announcement that all four original members would be reforming for a huge summer concert at London's Hyde Park came as a real surprise. It transpired that Graham saw Damon at an Africa Express concert in October, and finally – over tea and Eccles cake – the oldest of friends buried their seven-year hatchet.

With a rapidly-expanding schedule including an extra Hyde Park date, a UK tour and a Glastonbury Festival headline slot, the summer of 2009 was a giddily-triumphant return to the live arena for Britpop's favourite sons. The one-off single 'Fool's Day' followed in 2010, before the band reunited again in 2012 for the London Olympics closing-ceremony concert. Fans were also treated to another new single – 'Under the Westway' – and in 2013, Blur performed their first overseas gigs in a decade.

Contemporary Tracks

'Fool's Day' (Albarn, Coxon, James, Rowntree)

Single released 17 April 2010

Following Blur's glorious and galvanising summer 2009 reunion shows, it was decided in early-2010 that they would record an exclusive new track for Record Store Day. The single was the first Blur release since 'Music Is My Radar' to include Graham back on guitar duties. Far from being a big, shiny comeback smash, 'Fool's Day' (i.e. 1 April) is a chorus-less low-key affair that acts as an important bridge between former glories and the band's successful studio reincarnation on *The Magic Whip.*

Built on a minor-key groove with a melody recalling Cutting Crew's '(I Just) Died in Your Arms', this touching self-referential song chronicles the process of Blur finally patching up their musical differences. Damon's lyric paints a humdrum picture of waking up, eating porridge, taking his kid to school and heading down to the studio to make 'sweet music', and there are geographical shout-outs to the Westway and Ladbroke Grove, significant landmarks in his personal and professional life.

Being Graham's first Blur recording in a decade, he keeps things relatively sedate throughout, though there are glimpses of his former axe heroics, notably in the intro's swooshy atmospherics and his agile bluesy licks that take centre stage from 2:35. Unavailable on streaming services to this day, copies of the original 'Fool's Day' limited edition 7" single are now considered a collector's item.

'Under the Westway' (Albarn, Coxon, James, Rowntree)

Single released 2 July 2012. UK: 34

When Blur were offered the chance to headline the 2012 Olympics closing ceremony show at Hyde Park, Damon wrote the majestic ballad 'Under the Westway', especially for the momentous occasion. The Westway – a section of the A40 – is an elevated dual carriageway in and out of the West London suburbs. 'For Tomorrow' and, more recently 'Fool's Day' made lyrical allusions to it.

Damon and Graham originally performed 'Under the Westway' at the War Child benefit show at Brixton Academy in February 2012, and it was first attempted in the studio with *13* producer William Orbit. However, the sessions were abandoned after the band deemed Orbit's plodding and flippant arrangement to be unsatisfactory, Graham going as far as calling it 'an abomination'. Thankfully, Blur self-produced a superior rendition (mixed by Stephen Sedgwick) that became the definitive version.

With its atmospherically-delayed guitar chug and synth percussion crashes, the track opens like a sister piece to the 1980 Ultravox smash 'Vienna'. Then after an elegiacal piano, handbells, timpani and a two-note guitar intro, Damon begins singing:

There were blue skies in my city today
Everything was sinking
Said snow would come on Sunday
The old school was due and the traffic grew
Upon the Westway

Evocative and emotional, the verses poignantly ruminate on a host of topics, such as capitalism ('Men in yellow jackets putting adverts inside my dreams'), technology ('Bring us the day they switch off the machines') and a 'London Loves'-type reference to a game of darts ('Magic arrows hitting the bull').

The song resides in the same lighters-in-the-air space as rock classics like Procul Harum's 'A Whiter Shade of Pale' and The Beatles' 'Let It Be' – possessing a mournful descending piano-chord sequence and pretty 'aaah' Beach Boys-like backing vocals behind Graham's brief guitar solo. Damon's lead vocal is cut from the same heart-wrenching cloth as past tearjerkers like 'Best Days' and 'To the End', which – combined with the chamber-pop instrumentation – culminates in a grandiose form of sentimentality.

A beautiful addition to Blur's bittersweet ballad box, perhaps the biggest parallel that could be drawn here is with The Kinks' 'Waterloo Sunset' – Ray Davies' 1967 masterpiece being the natural precursor to this picturesque and geographic form of London balladry. Indeed, Davies had a profound influence on Damon's writing in the mid-1990s, a Blur period that this song warmly evokes.

'The Puritan' (Albarn, Coxon, James, Rowntree)

B-side of 'Under the Westway'

This song and its A-side were given their live debut on 2 July 2012 at a gig on studio 13's rooftop terrace. Live-streamed via Twitter, the performance coincided with the single's digital release later that same day.

With a jerky, stuttering pulse and a biting vocal, 'The Puritan' is a million miles from the elegant beauty of 'Under the Westway'. The quirky arrangement opens in disorienting fashion with a polyrhythm between a drum machine in 7/4 and a staccato keyboard phrase in 4/4. Other strange touches include the bass-synth part during the dubstep-lite chorus, mixed so loudly as to almost render the other instruments inconsequential. Elsewhere, the rascally 'la la la' vocals bring a welcome element of familiarity, as does Graham's raucous chorus guitar-thrashing, making up for the stiff rhythm section's lack of spontaneity.

Damon's oblique lyric appears to address the numb unconsciousness of modern times:

> It's smoke and it's mirrors
> Until the autocue starts
> Then the dry ice comes
> And we start sucking our thumbs on the TV
> And the joy of people
> Spirited away so merrily

These scornful lines might also be a reaction to Blur's February 2012 Brit Awards performance, which saw them criticised for an earthy and authentic showing, at odds with the manufactured sanitation of the era's typical mainstream acts. The song title – which alludes to cleansing the mainstream of the dirty impurities of real art – also seems to espouse this theory.

NME
SPECIAL COLLECTOR'S EDITION
Blur
The full story of Britain's greatest modern pop band
Baggy,
Britpop
and beyond
Celebrating
20 years of
Parklife
CHERYL
Blur vs Oasis:
The battle in full
Classic
interviews
Brand new
features
Every record
reassessed
And... will there finally be a new album?

The Magic Whip (2015)

Personnel:
Damon Albarn: Vocals, Keyboards, Acoustic Guitar, Melodica, Synthesizer, iPad
Graham Coxon: Guitars, Backing vocals, Co-lead vocals on 'Lonesome Street' and 'Thought I Was a Spaceman'
Alex James: Bass
Dave Rowntree: Drums, Percussion
Stephen Street: Programming, Percussion, Drum machine, Synth Sax on 'Ghost Ship'
James Dring: Drum programming
Demon Strings: Orchestration
Recorded May 2013 and November 2014-January 2015
Studios: Avon (Hong Kong); The Bunker, Miloco, 13 (London)
Producers: Stephen Street, Graham Coxon, Damon Albarn
Mixing: Stephen Street, Stephen Sedgwick
Release dates: UK: 27 April 2015, US: 28 April 2015
Label: Parlophone/UMG (UK), Warner Bros. (US)
Chart Placings: UK: 1, US: 24

Plans for an eighth Blur album had been in the works since 2012, with Damon having written new material for the upcoming Olympics closing ceremony. Hiring William Orbit to oversee the recordings (including 'Under the Westway'), Damon apparently halted the sessions in March that year. A spurned Orbit took to Twitter a few months later, venting his frustration over the abandoned work, calling Damon 'kinda a shit to the rest of Blur'. But band relations seemed good in this period, Blur subsequently undertaking a lengthy world tour in 2013, capitalising on their second reformation.

When the May 2013 Tokyo Rocks festival was cancelled, the guys remained in Hong Kong to wait for their next engagement, an Indonesian festival a week later. Ever the workaholic, Damon suggested they use this downtime to attempt recording a new album. An intense five-day session at Avon Studios ensued, with Stephen Sedgwick (Damon's Studio 13 in-house engineer) being flown out to collect the recordings and take them back to London. Despite recording fifteen new tracks, the songs were structurally and lyrically incomplete, and due to Blur's busy schedule, the recordings were filed away, presumably for good.

Fast-forward to October 2014, with Damon busy promoting his debut solo album *Everyday Robots*, it was Graham who expressed a desire to revisit the material. He confessed to *The Guardian* in 2015: 'I kept thinking about the recordings we had made in Hong Kong, and remembering how good it felt. I wouldn't have forgiven myself if I hadn't had another look.'

With Damon's blessing, Graham felt that Stephen Street was the man to help sift through the hours of music, and the two spent several weeks in November knocking the songs into shape at Street's South London studio, The Bunker.

After nervously presenting the work to Damon, thankfully, it was met with his seal of approval.

Having solo promo duties booked in Australia for December, Damon admirably revisited Hong Kong on his way back, acquiring inspiration for a marathon lyric-writing session over Christmas, while the others reconvened in the studio to complete their instrumental bits. In January at Studio 13, Damon recorded his vocals with Street, and the album was complete by the end of the month.

Managing to keep the album a total secret from the wider world, fans were ecstatic and stunned when on 19 February 2015, Blur held a press conference to announce the new album: their first as a foursome in sixteen years. Topping the UK charts and reaching high positions all over the world, the record was also critically well-received across the board as a creatively vibrant yet mature work – a late-marriage miracle baby worthy of standing alongside Blur's best work.

'Lonesome Street' (Albarn, Coxon, James, Rowntree)

Album preview single. Released 2 April 2015. UK: 151

The opening number is an unashamed return to the familiar stomp of Blur's mid-1990s Britpop pomp. With a title that you could jokingly attribute to Blur's outcast producer, jettisoned before the *13* sessions began, 'Lonesome Street' was the first track that Graham and Stephen Street played for Damon after completing the first round of post-production on the original Hong Kong tapes.

Bouncing along on a taut, spiky guitar riff, it's a highly pleasurable self-pastiche, with the verses featuring a reappropriation of Damon's cheeky, chirpy *Parklife*-era vocal style. Here we see him take a now-trademark swipe at the chaotic speed and frivolity of modern life:

> What do you got?
> Mass produced in somewhere hot
> You'll have to go on the Underground
> To get things done here

The verse two line, '5.14 to East Grinstead', came to Damon in the Hong Kong sessions and was kept in favour of a more topical lyric in tribute to friends of the band from Sussex, back in the 1990s. The soft lulling bridge sections boast stacked triad harmonies that gently fall like sunset. There's also Graham's beautiful jazz-like chords, not to mention Damon's compassionate vocal:

> And if you have nobody left to rely on
> I'll hold you in my arms and let you drift
> It's got to be that time again
> And June, June will be over soon again

In much the same vein as 'Tender', one key segment has Graham singing, doing his best Syd Barrett impression. Speaking to *NME* in 2015, he described the nursery-rhyme-like sequence:

> When I was listening back to it with Stephen, I thought, 'Why not go the whole hog and have a really Syd Barrett-y middle eight in there?'. So I wrote another section for it, which is about the way you seem to ride the tarmac in Hong Kong – you stand on the road, you don't move, and it will take you anywhere you want to go.

Spoken-word samples from the urban metropolis, pepper the arrangement, echoing the radio traffic reports on 'London Loves'. A jaunty coda – with burbling synths and a knees-up style whistling section – adds to the overall cheer.

Released as a digital single almost a month ahead of the album, this was perhaps *the* track that had fans of the Britpop glory days licking their lips in anticipation. In a bizarre twist of fate, Oasis frontman and longtime Blur adversary Liam Gallagher took to Twitter to name 'Lonesome Street' 'Song of the year'.

'New World Towers' (Albarn, Coxon, James, Rowntree)

Named after a 43-storey multipurpose skyscraper that Damon encountered in the heart of central Hong Kong, 'New World Towers' is a gentle, hazy tune that comes off like a sister song to those on his solo album *Everyday Robots*.

Set to a sound bed of minor-chord synths and sci-fi sound effects, Damon's desolate vocal conjures poetic imagery of a serene but bleak future:

> Green, green, the neon green, new world towers
> Plane flying overhead, satellite showers
> Fall like confetti on the cavalcade

Despite the lyric drawing on the cold corporate climate of today's major cities, Graham claims that none of this was on his mind when he and Stephen Street worked on the backing track, as there were no words or vocals to consider. Instead, he wanted it to sound like a 'science fiction Greensleeves', an endeavour you can hear in the Old English pastoral flute flourishes and pentatonic guitar phrases. Add Dave's soft trip-hop-ish brush drums and Alex's dub-reggae bass, and the elements combine to create a strangely peaceful dystopian affair reflecting the modern world's icy loneliness.

'Go Out' (Albarn, Coxon, James, Rowntree)

Album preview single. Released 19 February 2015. UK: 182

With its skronky swagger and abrasive guitar textures, 'Go Out' was the track that really got Damon excited when Graham and Stephen played him their works-in-progress in November 2015. Accordingly, it became the first thing the world heard from *The Magic Whip*, released in February 2015 as the album's first single.

Describing its genesis in the *Made in Hong Kong* making-of documentary, Damon asserted the track was a '6:30 in the afternoon song, and a lot dirtier than anything we'd recorded in the past'. In the same film, Alex elaborated further:

> We'd never be able to produce that if we went into a posh studio thinking 'We must write the lead track for the new Blur album'. Just because it's so relaxed, dirty and gritty, it suddenly makes it sound like Blur again. We're best when we're not trying too hard.

Creeping up on a squall of guitar feedback, the track settles into its fiendishly filthy groove early – reminiscent of an older, meaner 'London Loves'. Dave provides a solid, mooching drum pattern, while Alex's sliding bass riff rumbles menacingly in the lower frequencies. Damon's speak-sung vocal delivers lyrics that once again home in on loneliness and isolation in the urban jungle, featuring 'seedy western men' and 'greedy go-getters' who 'do it with themselves' after going out to 'the local'.

Graham is the track's standout performer, liberally spraying a plethora of deranged, mangled and distorted guitar phrases over the record, harking back to some of the more aggressive moments on *13*. It's by no means his most melodic Blur performance, but it is sonically electrifying like he's fawning over his effect pedals in a wrestling match with a seriously jealous guitar.

'Ice Cream Man' (Albarn, Coxon, James, Rowntree)

This offering is far more sinister than its title and cheerful strut suggests. It's the album's first reference to China's repressive past – buried in seemingly innocuous wordplay slyly referencing state control and – rumour has it – the 1989 Tiananmen Square protests:

> Here comes the ice cream man
> Parked at the end of the road
> With a swish of his magic whip
> All the people in the party froze
> I was only twenty-one
> When I watched it on T.V.
> I was racing in my heart

Damon explained the lyric further to *Billboard* in 2015: 'The sinister ice cream man with his white gloves. I set him in context of the protest. He's a policeman, and the whip is the state control. But the ice cream man is really sinister.'

The instrumentation is built on a strange blooping electronic loop that was a GarageBand demo sitting on Damon's iPad. Graham and Stephen Street took it and assembled a chorus from Damon's improvised demo vocals. Dave's soft brush kit and Graham's simple but taut acoustic guitar chords bring the arrangement back into Blur territory, with Alex's melodic bass part to the fore at 1:32. According to Graham, this bass solo of sorts was partly modelled on the Mr Softy theme tune that blared from every ice cream van up and down the country when they were kids in the 1970s.

This lyric also provided the album title. The eponymous firecracker that Damon encountered in Iceland on New Year's Eve 2014, tied in nicely with the lyric's themes.

'Thought I Was a Spaceman' (Albarn, Coxon, James, Rowntree)

At 6:16 in length, the album's longest track is also its most linear composition. The song keeps within its narrow structural framework, building slowly from a gentle drum machine opening (with Damon on acoustic guitar) to a soaring finale in which Graham takes the baton on lead vocals.

Coming on like Gorillaz rewriting David Bowie's 'Space Oddity', the song's thematic thrust centres around the twin states of isolation and alienation, which stem from Damon's return trip to Hong Kong in December 2014. He explained in the *Made In Hong Kong* documentary:

> I decided to go back on my own to Hong Kong, I was there for a day and a half. I got off the plane and started writing and filming. I felt a bit like a spaceman, and I started to take on dystopian levels of personal isolation, angst and fear. It all got quite intense, but that's really helpful when you're writing.

The lyric describes Damon as a sand-dune-dwelling spaceman, fighting to 'Keep the demons in'. He mentions the 'fight for Happy Valley' – a residential district of Hong Kong – and his spaceship's 'black box', washed-up on the outlying islands. Eventually, the spaceman winds up in Hyde Park, the scene of Blur's triumphant 2009 and 2012 reunion shows.

The lyric's spacey scenario is amplified through the astronautical arrangement, which contains dialogue from the 1969 moon-landing (4.28), and a xylophone synth riff recalling The Prodigy's 1992 hit 'Out of Space'. Graham's epic ascending guitar solo brings the piece to its climax, leading the spaceman to his final resting place.

'I Broadcast' (Albarn, Coxon, James, Rowntree)

Digital single. Released 21 April 2015

One of the album's final additions, this was recorded entirely in London. Again based on one of Damon's iPad demos, it's a result of needing a faster, punky number. But there's none of the reckless abandon that characterised the likes of 'Chinese Bombs', 'Bugman' or 'Bank Holiday' here. Instead, it's a polished and sanitised piece, benefitting from a nifty arrangement that

– thanks to Damon's retro synth lines – suggests a 1980s arcade machine covering 'Popscene'.

The drums are tight and sticky, with a lively groove beneath Alex's melodic and peppy bass line. Graham is at his inventive best, starting with jarring, sliding chord stabs, delivering high-pitched string-dampened guitar chugging in the verses and snaking distorted licks in the post-chorus sections.

Damon's vocal is speak-sung with the same bratty Britpop sneer as the aforementioned 'Popscene', spitting out lyrics that Graham claims are about 'going to different places and the people there know a lot about you, even though you don't think they do'.

I love the aspects of another city
It's got your number and your blood type
They been intentious so need some focus
The apparitions of another prodigal night, right?

These words could also be seen to reflect how the internet, mass surveillance and other new technology forms make the world more intertwined, with your vital information indexed in some far away computer. Either way, 'I Broadcast' is entertaining and energetic – administering a welcome shot of adrenaline to an otherwise mid-tempo record.

'My Terracotta Heart' (Albarn, Coxon, James, Rowntree)

Digital single. Released 18 April 2015

Towards the end of Blur's five-day 2013 Hong Kong recording session, Graham had – in Damon's words – 'a wobble'. What transpired has not been divulged, but regardless, this would've been a concerning development for all involved, no doubt bringing back memories of Graham's departure when recording *Think Tank.* This inspired Damon to write 'My Terracotta Heart'.

With the word 'terracotta' being a metaphor for the brittle nature of the two protagonists' emotions, the song is a mournful ballad verging on smooth soft-rock sounds. Damon's heartfelt vocal is forlorn, passionate and sadly looks back to a time when the two were much closer ('We were more like brothers, but that was years ago'). The brokenhearted chorus laments this sense of loss. 'It's about giving someone a second and a third chance at friendship,' Damon later explained, 'and then they blow it again and you're wondering if you can take any more'.

I'm running out of heart today
I'm running out of open road to you
And I know you are emoting and you're dazed
Is something broke inside you?
'Cause at the moment I'm lost
And feeling that I don't know if I'm losing you again

The arrangement has an elegant poise, with Graham's soulful, clean guitar tone to the fore, providing serene licks with bluesy string bends. Talking to the *NME* in 2015, he explained his thinking: 'I knew it was going to be an incredibly sad song, which is why I put that crying guitar on there. What I didn't know at the time, was that the lyrics would turn out to be about Damon and I, our long friendship and the ups and downs we've had.'

But Graham isn't the only one in top form here, with Alex's bass-playing being exquisite. His dextrous and delicate chorus runs propel the song forward, dovetailing well with Graham's coda guitar part. It ends with Damon self-harmonising in three-part.

'There Are Too Many of Us' (Albarn, Coxon, James, Rowntree)

Digital single. Released 20 March 2015

Arguably the album's bleakest track, this was partly inspired by the Sydney Lindt Cafe siege, which Damon witnessed while touring his solo LP *Everyday Robots* in December 2014. In a 2015 interview with Australia's *ABC News*, he explained the situation:

> I was staying in a hotel, which was like a block away from the square. Outside of the window, everything was very normal and unexceptional, but on the television, it was like World War III was about to break out. The song is influenced by that sort of mad distortion that takes place on these sort of events.

Notwithstanding the one verse which mentions being distracted by 'terror on a loop elsewhere', the lyrics focus more – as the title suggests – on overpopulation, which Graham has since confirmed was a result of their stay in Hong Kong. Here, he ruminates on the notion that we are all obsessed with our own self-importance whilst lamenting society's encouragement to create new families:

> There are too many of us
> That's plain to see
> We all believe in praying
> For our immortality
>
> We pose this question to our children
> That calls them all to stray
> And live in tiny houses
> Of the same mistakes we make

With such heavy subject matter, the arrangement is suitably dour, featuring Dave's military drum pattern and some 'Cloudbusting'-esque minor-chord staccato string stabs, courtesy of the Demon Strings (Damon's in-house string group). Some echoing garbled speech appears at 1:28, and the track takes an ominous totalitarian turn, perhaps influenced by Damon's time in North Korea.

Though Graham plays guitar here – acoustic and a brief solo – his main contribution was – in his words – the 'big fat death-ray laser sounds', best heard in the synth-dominated middle section.

'Ghost Ship' (Albarn, Coxon, James, Rowntree)

Though *The Magic Whip* often returns to genres and themes that Blur (and occasionally Gorillaz) had previously explored, 'Ghost Ship' is a first for the group, a luxurious, swooning lilt that Damon proudly describes as 'compass-point blue-eyed soul'.

Opening with Dave's chilled-out Specials 'Ghost Town' drums and Stax-ish saxophone stabs (courtesy of Stephen Street's samples), the soul influence is all over this arrangement. Alex gets to play out his James Jamerson fantasies with a thrusting Motown bassline before Graham arrives with a clean Curtis Mayfield-type guitar tone on plenty of sliding bluesy licks and major-7 chords. Damon's vocal croon is melodious and warm, backing himself with syrupy three-part 'aaah''s on the bridges, while celesta and Rhodes piano parts are sprinkled like sugar over a cake.

Again featuring allusions to Hong Kong (there's a mention of the Po Lin Buddhist monastery), Damon's lyric is tender and personal, pining for an unidentified loved one:

Till I ever hold you out there again, will you be mine?
'Cause I'm on a ghost ship, drowning my heart in Hong Kong
It's the last ride boarding here tonight
Out in the bay
I'll need a lantern in you to shine out bright rays

Verse one nods to the album title, while the lines 'I got away, for a little while / But then it came back much harder' could be describing how intense the lure of the Chinese territory became on Damon's second stay there.

Despite Graham opining 'Ghost Ship' to be 'very much a Damon song', it has subsequently become something of an unexpected hit for the band. Having racked up close to 50,000,000 hits, it currently sits in Blur's top 10 streamed Spotify tracks, above such classics as 'Country House', 'Beetlebum' and 'The Universal' – not bad for a song that was given neither an official single release nor video.

'Pyongyang' (Albarn, Coxon, James, Rowntree)

This grandiose epic ode to North Korea's capital city (and *The Magic Whip*'s undoubted showstopper) was born after Damon visited Pyongyang in 2013 while conceptualising his involvement in composing the *Wonder.land* musical. Speaking to *GQ* about his time there, he recalled:

> When you go there, I can best describe it as a magical kingdom, in the sense that everyone is under a spell. The statues and the edifices are absolutely everywhere – everywhere you go, you're reminded of the Kim family. They are truly omnipresent.

Though the city made quite an impression on Damon, the song itself was nowhere near finished when Graham and Stephen Street began work on the original demo in November 2014. Graham reports that the song was merely a 'bleak dirge' with no melody present in the chorus. Accordingly, he composed one himself – briefly featured in the final chorus (at 4:09) as an overlapping vocal counterpoint to Damon's eventual lead part.

> Kid the mausoleum's fallen
> And the perfect avenues
> Will seem empty without you
> And the pink light that bathes the great leaders is fading
> By the time your sun is rising there
> Out here it's turning blue
> The silver rocket's coming
> And the cherry trees of Pyongyang
> But I'm leaving

Damon spent a day in Pyongyang visiting the mausoleum of the great leaders, and later explained that the lyrics were meant as a postcard home to his daughter on the last day of the regime, telling her that he's getting out and coming home.

Brooding and studiously serious, the piece is reminiscent of Berlin-period Bowie, although it most specifically resembles the *Scary Monsters* cut 'Ashes to Ashes'. Built on a slow, mournful bossa nova groove, the cool atmosphere is heightened through woozy synths, icy electronic squiggles and vibrato guitar twangs, whilst Damon's vocal flits between the verse's sombre baritone whisper and the chorus' impassioned and belting top-of-the-chest register.

One can't talk about this song without mentioning its unusual harmonic structure. The sombre verses are rooted in the key of C minor, though the choruses make an unexpected move up a minor third to Eb minor. However, it seems that the actual key of this section is B major, implied by its dominant (or V) chord being F#, on the lyric 'but I'm leaving'. Then, in the fade, the harmony settles on a looping transition between a minor and major F# chord, which is the piece's third key change.

'Ong Ong' (Albarn, Coxon, James, Rowntree)

Digital single. Released 23 April 2015

This began life four years earlier as a GarageBand sketch, and was whipped out late in the day during sessions at Avon Studios. A beers-in-the-air sing-along single, the title came from a strange noise at the beginning of the demo. Apparently 'symbolic of the serendipity of the record', Damon realised that if he put an H and a K at the beginning of each Ong, you'd get Hong Kong.

It's a three-chord mid-tempo chugger, replete with 'la-la-la' group vocals. The central 'I wanna be with you' line is a universally popular theme, up there with 'Always should be someone you really love'. Enhanced by the steel drum keyboards, the mood is sun-soaked and tropical, reminding Graham of 'being on a beach with palm trees swaying'. Accordingly, his guitar-playing takes on a distinctly Hawaiian/Calypso bent: all 6th chords, string bends and slides. Speaking to the *NME* in 2015, he said, 'It's like some kind of weird advert for the Bahamas. I really like it, but sometimes a song will ask some weird stuff of you – stuff that you might not necessarily like doing, but the song has told you to do it, and so you have to obey!'

Damon's vocal melody is seductive and simple, mainly sticking to two notes, but veering dangerously close to the 'All of the time, well I'm never sure why I need you' line from 'Song 2'. The performance itself is crisp and restrained, so much so that the band perhaps could've done with a little more raucousness (particularly in the gang vocals, which land a little flat) to counter the jaunty, jovial atmosphere.

'Mirrorball' (Albarn, Coxon, James, Rowntree)

This desert-rock-infused number closes the album in melancholic fashion, Alex claiming it was already fully formed on Damon's demo. Again thematically centred in Hong Kong, verse one references the locations Ocean Park and Jordan Train Station – the latter being where the band would disembark en route to Avon Studios. Verse two talks of the Umbrella Revolution protests that took place from September to December 2014:

> I'll be back when December comes
> All the barriers have been pulled down
> Where is everyone?

At Damon's own admission, the yearning chorus was written from the perspective of talking to his then-teenage daughter Missy online while travelling:

> So before you log out
> Hold close to me

Graham heightens the drama by providing Link-Ray-inspired reverb-drenched twanging guitar textures, courtesy of a recently acquired custom-built Stratocaster with tremolo arm. Add some 'Miss America'-style woodblock and the Demon Strings' dark and haunting eastern-flavoured phrases, and we have an atmosphere akin to a Sergio Leone western shot in Asia. Incidentally, it's a style Graham had dabbled with on 'Are You Ready' from his 2004 album *Happiness in Magazines*. Fans of Welsh psych-pop legends Super Furry Animals may also notice the similarity between the vocal and guitar melody here, to the main vocal and instrumental melody on their track 'Sarn Helen'.

Contemporary Tracks

'Y'all Doomed' (Albarn, Coxon, James, Rowntree)

Limited-edition single. Released 27 April 2015 Also Japanese bonus track on The Magic Whip.

The playfully experimental 'Y'all Doomed' was recorded during the five-day sessions at Hong Kong's Avon Studios. A piece of two halves, the first is a kooky dub-reggae jam with a pitch-shifted Damon vocal repeatedly uttering the title. Things reach a higher gear when the band start playing an up-tempo motorik groove. This time, Graham takes a vocal, following Damon's lead by chanting the single phrase 'I need another nation'. Machine-like delay-pedal guitar textures follow before the band finally explode into a zany punk blast to finish – offering a tantalising glimpse of what might've been had they taken a similar approach on the *13* track 'Trailerpark'.

Epilogue

Now that the dust has settled on *The Magic Whip* – and with all four members going back to their separate lives and careers – one can't help but pose the question: have Blur really 'made it to the end'? Other than an impromptu appearance during a March 2019 Africa Express gig, the band haven't officially performed together since the Abu Dhabi Grand Prix after-race concert in November 2015. Damon has recently been quoted in the NME, saying the guys have 'had a chat' about an idea for a reunion, but it seems that that's as far as things have gone, and whether or not this would involve new material, is anyone's guess. With all this in mind, perhaps the moment is ripe for a reappraisal of one of the UK's most successful and best-loved bands of the last 30 years.

From humble beginnings as inexperienced indie hopefuls, becoming Britain's biggest pop group; reinventing themselves as experimental pioneers, and eventually becoming treasured elder statesmen, Blur have had the most extraordinary of journeys. Indeed, perhaps the most impressive element of their story is the thematic range and sheer musical scope covered across those eight albums, 34 singles and over 70 original B-sides. Though not as commercially successful as Oasis, nor as critically revered as Radiohead, Blur covered more ground than either, exploring such disparate areas of the musical palette as dance rock, synth-pop, gospel, electronica, punk, grunge, psychedelia, music hall, worldbeat, lo-fi, dub, blue-eyed soul; the list goes on. Not only did they do all this, they did it brilliantly, with invention and integrity, while still sounding like Blur.

Of course, this couldn't have happened without the individual personnel. In Damon Albarn, Blur possessed arguably the greatest songwriter of a generation – his evolution over the course of Blur's career showing fascinating snapshots of a man traversing numerous life changes and progressions in taste. After an unsure and confused beginning, his talent blossomed in the Britpop years, deploying concise and clever wordplay portraying a plethora of alternating moods – humorous, poignant, rousing, melancholic, biting. He utterly nailed the art of observational storytelling. In Blur's late-1990s volte-face, his writing took on a new maturity – becoming heartfelt, confessional and often abstract, you got the sense that there was nothing he couldn't turn his hand to. This was all wrapped up with a supreme gift for melody and harmony, surpassing many of his contemporaries.

Like Damon's songwriting, Graham's guitar talents are virtually peerless. Intense yet impossibly deft, his mastery of effects pedals and sonics is astounding – the dexterity and invention of his most complex parts often leave the listener breathless. Stephen Street was once quoted as saying that Graham's work surpassed that of The Smith's Johnny Marr, while Radiohead's Jonny Greenwood has on numerous occasions spoken in awe of Graham's work.

Then there's the rhythm section. Alex has to be the most underrated bass player around: simultaneously funky, melodic, heavy and robust; he's got it all. Similarly, Dave as a drummer is world-class. Though often given the task of keeping impeccable time, his playing is tastefully supple, and when called upon, he always pulls heroics out of the bag. The chemistry of these four characters with their unrivalled skill-sets created a special kind of magic. No wonder Beck called them 'The other fab four' on his Instagram page in 2015.

Regrettably – and despite the huge contribution they made to the fabric of popular music in the 1990s – it seems that Blur are the last of a dying breed. Thanks to the sad state of affairs the music industry has gradually sunken into over the last fifteen years, there hasn't been a single band emerge in that time that could lay claim to Blur's stylistic diversity, musical intelligence and cultural impact. Today, musicians are musicians, artists are artists, and pop stars are pop stars, and rarely do they crossbreed, like all the best used to. In that sense, Blur were graced with the perfect name.

On Track series

Tori Amos – Lisa Torem 978-1-78952-142-9
Asia – Peter Braidis 978-1-78952-099-6
Barclay James Harvest – Keith and Monica Domone 978-1-78952-067-5
The Beatles – Andrew Wild 978-1-78952-009-5
The Beatles Solo 1969-1980 – Andrew Wild 978-1-78952-030-9
Blue Oyster Cult – Jacob Holm-Lupo 978-1-78952-007-1
Marc Bolan and T.Rex – Peter Gallagher 978-1-78952-124-5
Kate Bush – Bill Thomas 978-1-78952-097-2
Camel – Hamish Kuzminski 978-1-78952-040-8
Caravan – Andy Boot 978-1-78952-127-6
Cardiacs – Eric Benac 978-1-78952-131-3
Eric Clapton Solo – Andrew Wild 978-1-78952-141-2
The Clash – Nick Assirati 978-1-78952-077-4
Crosby, Stills and Nash – Andrew Wild 978-1-78952-039-2
The Damned – Morgan Brown 978-1-78952-136-8
Deep Purple and Rainbow 1968-79 – Steve Pilkington 978-1-78952-002-6
Dire Straits – Andrew Wild 978-1-78952-044-6
The Doors – Tony Thompson 978-1-78952-137-5
Dream Theater – Jordan Blum 978-1-78952-050-7
Elvis Costello and The Attractions – Georg Purvis 978-1-78952-129-0
Emerson Lake and Palmer – Mike Goode 978-1-78952-000-2
Fairport Convention – Kevan Furbank 978-1-78952-051-4
Peter Gabriel – Graeme Scarfe 978-1-78952-138-2
Genesis – Stuart MacFarlane 978-1-78952-005-7
Gentle Giant – Gary Steel 978-1-78952-058-3
Gong – Kevan Furbank 978-1-78952-082-8
Hawkwind – Duncan Harris 978-1-78952-052-1
Roy Harper – Opher Goodwin 978-1-78952-130-6
Iron Maiden – Steve Pilkington 978-1-78952-061-3
Jefferson Airplane – Richard Butterworth 978-1-78952-143-6
Jethro Tull – Jordan Blum 978-1-78952-016-3
Elton John in the 1970s – Peter Kearns 978-1-78952-034-7
The Incredible String Band – Tim Moon 978-1-78952-107-8
Iron Maiden – Steve Pilkington 978-1-78952-061-3
Judas Priest – John Tucker 978-1-78952-018-7
Kansas – Kevin Cummings 978-1-78952-057-6
Led Zeppelin – Steve Pilkington 978-1-78952-151-1
Level 42 – Matt Philips 978-1-78952-102-3
Aimee Mann – Jez Rowden 978-1-78952-036-1
Joni Mitchell – Peter Kearns 978-1-78952-081-1
The Moody Blues – Geoffrey Feakes 978-1-78952-042-2
Mike Oldfield – Ryan Yard 978-1-78952-060-6
Tom Petty – Richard James 978-1-78952-128-3

Porcupine Tree – Nick Holmes 978-1-78952-144-3
Queen – Andrew Wild 978-1-78952-003-3
Radiohead – William Allen 978-1-78952-149-8
Renaissance – David Detmer 978-1-78952-062-0
The Rolling Stones 1963-80 – Steve Pilkington 978-1-78952-017-0
The Smiths and Morrissey – Tommy Gunnarsson 978-1-78952-140-5
Steely Dan – Jez Rowden 978-1-78952-043-9
Steve Hackett – Geoffrey Feakes 978-1-78952-098-9
Thin Lizzy – Graeme Stroud 978-1-78952-064-4
Toto – Jacob Holm-Lupo 978-1-78952-019-4
U2 – Eoghan Lyng 978-1-78952-078-1
UFO – Richard James 978-1-78952-073-6
The Who – Geoffrey Feakes 978-1-78952-076-7
Roy Wood and the Move – James R Turner 978-1-78952-008-8
Van Der Graaf Generator – Dan Coffey 978-1-78952-031-6
Yes – Stephen Lambe 978-1-78952-001-9
Frank Zappa 1966 to 1979 – Eric Benac 978-1-78952-033-0
10CC – Peter Kearns 978-1-78952-054-5

Decades Series

The Bee Gees in the 1960s – Andrew Mon Hughes et al 978-1-78952-148-1
Alice Cooper in the 1970s – Chris Sutton 978-1-78952-104-7
Curved Air in the 1970s – Laura Shenton 978-1-78952-069-9
Fleetwood Mac in the 1970s – Andrew Wild 978-1-78952-105-4
Focus in the 1970s – Stephen Lambe 978-1-78952-079-8
Genesis in the 1970s – Bill Thomas 978178952-146-7
Marillion in the 1980s – Nathaniel Webb 978-1-78952-065-1
Pink Floyd In The 1970s – Georg Purvis 978-1-78952-072-9
The Sweet in the 1970s – Darren Johnson 978-1-78952-139-9
Uriah Heep in the 1970s – Steve Pilkington 978-1-78952-103-0
Yes in the 1980s – Stephen Lambe with David Watkinson 978-1-78952-125-2

On Screen series

Carry On… – Stephen Lambe 978-1-78952-004-0
David Cronenberg – Patrick Chapman 978-1-78952-071-2
Doctor Who: The David Tennant Years – Jamie Hailstone 978-1-78952-066-8
Monty Python – Steve Pilkington 978-1-78952-047-7
Seinfeld Seasons 1 to 5 – Stephen Lambe 978-1-78952-012-5
James Bond – Andrew Wild 978-1-78952-010-1

Other Books

Babysitting A Band On The Rocks – G.D. Praetorius 978-1-78952-106-1
Derek Taylor: For Your Radioactive Children – Andrew Darlington 978-1-78952-038-5
Iggy and The Stooges On Stage 1967-1974 – Per Nilsen 978-1-78952-101-6
Jon Anderson and the Warriors – the road to Yes – David Watkinson 978-1-78952-059-0
Nu Metal: A Definitive Guide – Matt Karpe 978-1-78952-063-7
Tommy Bolin: In and Out of Deep Purple – Laura Shenton 978-1-78952-070-5
Maximum Darkness – Deke Leonard 978-1-78952-048-4
Maybe I Should've Stayed In Bed – Deke Leonard 978-1-78952-053-8
Psychedelic Rock in 1967 – Kevan Furbank 978-1-78952-155-9
The Twang Dynasty – Deke Leonard 978-1-78952-049-1

and many more to come!

Would you like to write for Sonicbond Publishing?

We are mainly a music publisher, but we also occasionally publish in other genres including film and television. At Sonicbond Publishing we are always on the look-out for authors, particularly for our two main series, On Track and Decades.

Mixing fact with in depth analysis, the On Track series examines the entire recorded work of a particular musical artist or group. All genres are considered from easy listening and jazz to 60s soul to 90s pop, via rock and metal.

The Decades series singles out a particular decade in an artist or group's history and focuses on that decade in more detail than may be allowed in the On Track series.

While professional writing experience would, of course, be an advantage, the most important qualification is to have real enthusiasm and knowledge of your subject. First-time authors are welcomed, but the ability to write well in English is essential.

Sonicbond Publishing has distribution throughout Europe and North America, and all our books are also published in E-book form. Authors will be paid a royalty based on sales of their book. Further details about our books are available from www.sonicbondpublishing.com. To contact us, complete the contact form there or email info@sonicbondpublishing.co.uk